Lorna

Message Received and Understood!

How to Communicate Effectively in Today's Business World

by
Helen Wilkie

MHW Communications
1999

Canadian Cataloguing in Publication Data
Wilkie, Helen, 1943 -
Message received and understood!

Includes index.
ISBN 0-9684626-0-X

1.Business communications. 2. Business writing. I. Title

HF5718.W544 1999 658.4'5 C98-933038-9

Distributed by:
MHW Communications
90 Warren Road, Suite 202,
Toronto, Ontario, Canada M4V 2S2
To order: (416) 966-5023

Cover art and book design by Felix Trindade
Edited by Ann Andrews

To Felix, the love of my life

Acknowledgements

Without the help and encouragement of a few very special people, this book would never have moved from the idea stage to the printed page. I acknowledge them below, with thanks and much appreciation.

My cousin, Chriss McCallum, who gave me the benefit of her own publishing experience and expertise, and put me on the right track from the beginning.

Ann Andrews, who made sure my subjects and verbs were all in agreement and curbed my tendency to overindulge in punctuation.

Lois Ferguson and Susan Birkenshaw, "The Butt Kickers", whose regular prodding, questioning and encouragement were invaluable, and who also helped me come up with the title.

Lastly—and most importantly—my husband, Felix Trindade. Not only did he give me his professional expertise in the design of the book, but he unfailingly gives me his loving support in everything I do.

To all these, my sincere thanks.

Helen Wilkie
Toronto
1999

Contents

Introduction .... *vii*

Helen's 9 Rules for Better Business Writing 11

Helen's 9 Rules for Pithy Presentations 39

Helen's 9 Rules for Lively Listening 73

Helen's 9 Rules for Meaningful Meetings 97

Helen's 9 Rules for Publishable Prose 123

In Closing 151

Introduction

Communication technology is burgeoning. Modern telecommunication bears little resemblance to the simple telephone invented by my fellow Scot, Alexander Graham Bell. Voicemail abounds. We flash messages around the globe in moments by e-mail. The Internet—well, the Internet simply boggles the mind.

So, with all these technological marvels available to us, why are we still not communicating? In performing needs analyses to find out how they can best help their employees, my corporate clients almost inevitably find communication skills to be desperately needed.

I believe the reason is that we are so caught up in the technology that we forget it is simply a *medium* for getting our message across. The message itself must still be created through use of the written and spoken word.

The Communication Contract©

American broadcaster and journalist Sydney J. Harris pointed out that although the words *information* and *communication* are often used interchangeably, they do not mean the same thing. Information, according to Harris, is giving out, while communication is getting through.

He was right. Another way of putting it is that there is no such thing as one-way communication. There is, of course, one-way information flow, but that's not the same thing at all. The principle of double-entry accounting tells us that for every debit there is a corresponding credit. In much the same way, for every piece of information that is outward bound there must be a corresponding receipt and understanding of that message before communication can be said to have taken place. I call this *The Communication Contract*©, and it's every bit as important as any other contract into which your organization enters. Here's how it works.

■ Writing is outward bound information. If you want to convey a message in writing, you must express it as clearly and concisely as possible, in language appropriate to your reader. That's the ***writer's*** part of the contract.

If you then send your letter to me, I must read it with enough concentration, attention and respect so that I receive the same message as you sent. That's the ***reader's*** part of the contract.

And unless both parties fulfil their parts, communication doesn't take place.

■ It's virtually impossible to succeed in a business career today without the ability to present effectively. You must speak with confidence, knowledge and power so that your message is clear. That's the ***speaker's*** part of the contract.

But the other side of oral communication is often under-rated: listening. As you make your presentation, I must **decide** to listen. That's not the same as having sound reverberate off my ear drums. That's hearing, and it's not at all the same function. I must listen with my ears, my eyes, often my body and always my mind, so that I receive and understand your message. That's the ***listener's*** part of the contract.

And unless both parties fulfil their parts, communication doesn't take place.

■ Individuals and organizations communicate without words all the time—through their actions and behaviour. Managers who always keep their office doors closed, for example, are sending a wordless message whether they realize it or not. Make sure your actions send the message you intend, because that's the ***behaviour*** part of the contract.

Those who observe those actions learn from them. If I submit suggestion after suggestion to my manager on how to improve my department's results but never receive any response or feedback, I learn that my ideas are not welcome. If at least a percentage of my ideas are used, then I learn that the manager is open to my contribution. That's the ***learning*** part of the contract.

And only when both sides fulfil their parts does communication truly take place.

In this book, I will give you what I call *Helen's 9 Rules* for the writing, presenting and listening skills. I also apply *Helen's 9 Rules* to two special communication situations: business meetings and writing articles for publication.

If you are offended by the word "rules", please understand that these are simply *my* rules. I have compiled them based on techniques which I have observed over the years to be helpful in raising the effectiveness of communication skills. They are the rules I follow, and they have made me a better communicator. I believe they will do the same for you.

Helen's 9 Rules for Better Business Writing

Many of the letters, memos and reports that pass for business correspondence today are a complete waste of time. They are a waste of time for those who wrote them, and they are certainly a waste of time for those who have to read and often interpret them. That's because they don't fulfil their primary objective, which is to communicate a message. That's the only reason to write anything in the business world—to communicate a message. The reason they fail is that often, quite inadvertently, the writer has erected barriers between the essence of the message and the reader's mind. So the message falls right down the middle, thus supporting George Bernard Shaw's observation, "The main problem with communication is the illusion that it has been accomplished."

Helen's 9 Rules for Better Business Writing is a series of tips and guidelines for communicating clearly and concisely through your correspondence.

Rule No. 1: Write for your reader

Too many business letters are written for the writer, not for the reader. The writer knows what he or she wants to say, but often uses language that is inappropriate for the reader for many reasons. When you sit down to write a letter, report or memo, ask yourself this short series of questions:

- Why am I writing this? What is the message I want to convey?
- Who is my audience for this particular piece of correspondence?
- What does this person want or need to know?
- How can I convey my message clearly and concisely?

By identifying your reader in your mind before you start, you can determine how you need to express yourself.

One of the main barriers to business communication is the inappropriate use of jargon. Is the reader a member of your company, your organization, your industry or profession? If so, a certain amount of jargon may be appropriate. After all, jargon comes into being simply because it is often the best means of communication among members of a particular group. The problem arises, however, when we forget that the person to whom we are writing is outside that group, and may not understand our special language.

For example, do you know what the following terms mean?

1. full bleed
2. GAAP
3. to die intestate
4. term life
5. laproscopic procedure

If you were a printer or graphic designer, you would know No. 1 means the ink covers the paper right to the edge of the sheet. An accountant would know No. 2 stands for Generally Accepted Accounting Principles. 3. Any lawyer could tell you No. 3 refers to a person who dies without making a will. To the insurance industry, No. 4 represents a type of insurance policy. Surgeons perform No. 5 when they make small incisions to carry out internal surgery with the help of computers and cameras. But if you don't belong to any of these professional groups you probably won't know the expressions, because they are jargon. Jargon is a special type of "insider" language designed to communicate easily with other members of a particular group. So there's no reason why you should know any of these terms, and you shouldn't expect others to understand *your* jargon either.

Imagine a cocktail party conversation involving a doctor, a lawyer, an engineer, a plumber, a commercial printer and a rock musician—all using their own professional jargon. What a babble that would produce! Nobody would understand anything that was going on. But that's exactly the effect you create when you use your professional jargon, your own special "in" language, to a reader outside the group. They won't understand, and if they don't understand the words you use, you have thrown up the first barrier to communication.

So remember, identify your audience before you start writing, and focus on their needs as you write.

Rule No. 2: Use simple words

Professionals, in particular, seem to have a problem with the idea of using simple words—I think they're afraid people will think they are not well-educated. But they won't, you know. If you use simple words, people won't notice them at all because they will be too busy getting the message. That's called communication, and it's the object of the exercise! On the next page are some examples of simple words you can substitute for complex ones.

Instead of		*Consider*
LOCATE	Why do business letters insist on *locating* files—or people—when normal conversation would just *find* them?	**FIND**
FURNISH	Imagine you come from another country and English is not your first language. How confused you would be seeing a word you associate with tables and chairs in the context of information movement!	**PROVIDE, GIVE**
TERMINATE	If you are in the legal profession, you may have to use this word in contracts and other legal documents. But don't carry it over to ordinary correspondence—it's much better to use the simpler word...	**END, FINISH**
OPTIMUM	Some simple words tend to fall into disuse because people think the fancier version sounds more important. You may be surprised to know that not everyone knows what *optimum* means. But everyone understands...	**BEST**
FORWARD	This verb is properly used to say something is sent from one person to another and then on to another. The first person in the chain, however, doesn't *forward* but merely *sends*.	**SEND**
CONCEPT	The advertising industry has raised this word to special status. When the client has an idea, it's just an idea. But the agency's idea becomes *The Concept*. A group of people sitting round a table throwing ideas around is usually said to be *brainstorming*. But when the ad agency people do it, it's called *conceptualization*—and it's very expensive!	**IDEA**

What simpler versions of the following words could you use?

Instead of	***Try***
utilize	____________________
parameters	____________________
paradigm	____________________
commencement	____________________
expedite	____________________
cognizant	____________________
diminutive	____________________
iteration	____________________

A colleague once inserted a meaningless string of these high-sounding words in a business memo. The grammatical construction was believable, but the sentence made no sense. Nobody noticed! We've become so used to skimming over words we don't immediately understand that we don't even notice the meaning. Is that communication? I don't think so. In fact, this is a classic example of a message sent but not received.

This doesn't mean you must never use a more complex word, but several in one sentence make for heavy reading. This automatically makes them a barrier to communication. So when there is a choice—and there almost always is—lean towards the simple word.

Rule No. 3: Cut out the fluff

Many a two page letter could be reduced to one page if we would just stop saying things like *in the majority of instances* when we mean *usually*. Why do we say *as you may or may not know*? Think about it. If you may know, then obviously you may not know. That's what *may* means. If you think they probably know, say *as you may know*. If you think they don't, say *as you may not know*, but you don't need the whole thing. Where did *at this point in time* come from? It seems to be some sort of attempt to bring cosmic significance to something quite ordinary! What's wrong with *at present*, or *now*?

People often use wordy phrases such as *of a confidential nature* instead of a perfectly good, serviceable adjective like *confidential*. The same applies to *historical, legal, private* and many others. When you can use a single word instead of a phrase, without losing any meaning, choose the word.

Here are a few more examples of common fluff that can easily be replaced.

Instead of	***Try***
10 a.m. in the morning	________________
try to attempt a solution	________________
proceeding in a westerly direction	________________
on a daily basis	________________
twenty-seven years of age	________________
it was red in colour	________________

Another common form of fluff is the phrase containing redundant words. One example is *new breakthrough*—have you ever heard of an old breakthrough? The word *breakthrough* stands on its own, and its meaning is clear. Here's another: *This young man has a great future ahead of him.* Where else would his future be but ahead? The other side of that is *past history*. History is, by definition, past—you don't need to define it again. And what about *the honest truth?* Is there another kind? We often write *very unique*. *Unique* is a word we have stolen from the French language—the least we can do is use it correctly. It doesn't mean *unusual*. It means there is only one. So something cannot be very unique, somewhat unique, rather unique or even quite unique. It might be very unusual—but it's either unique or it's not. And since it's in the nature of an emergency to take us by surprise, why do we say *unexpected emergency?*

Here are a few more to eliminate from your writing.

Instead of	***Try***
foreign import	____________________
absolutely perfect	____________________
necessary requisite	____________________
permission and approval	____________________
due and payable	____________________
the resulting consequence	____________________

Think twice next time you use any of these. When editing what you have written, look for instances where you have said the same thing twice, and take out the fluff.

Rule No. 4: Use gender neutral language

Fortunately, it seems we have gone beyond any argument as to whether we should be using gender neutral language in business. Most reasonable people agree we must. However, there are still questions as to the best ways of doing so. It does take a little extra effort, but here are a few relatively simple methods.

Sentence in plural form

Instead of:
Each employee must discuss his performance appraisal with his supervisor.

We could say:
All employees must discuss their performance appraisals with their supervisors.

In the first example, we use the masculine pronoun *his* twice. But if we talk of each *employee* in this context, we really mean all the employees, so why not use that expression? Then we can use the plural pronoun *their*, which is gender neutral. Be careful when you do this, though, that you keep the parts of the sentence in agreement. For example, if we leave the word *supervisor* in the singular, that would mean there was only one supervisor for all the employees.

Definite article instead of personal pronoun

The definite article is the word *the*.

Instead of:
The successful consultant always keeps his client's interests in mind.

We could say:
The successful consultant always keeps the client's interests in mind.

Plural pronoun in singular setting

This sounds confusing, and it is. It is also grammatically incorrect. However, despite this, it is worth discussing because the fact that it fulfils a need is rapidly making it acceptable to business writers.

Instead of:
Each executive is entitled to his own parking space.

We could say:
Each executive is entitled to their own parking space.

Language is not a static thing. It is a dynamic, growing body of words and phrases that is constantly changing in response to the needs of the society using it. That's why the English spoken in England is different from the English spoken in America. It's the reason Quebec French is different from Parisian French. The variations result from societies in different regions of the world adapting the language to suit their own particular needs. It is interesting that this use of the plural pronoun in the singular form was considered correct until the middle of the last century, when for some reason it became unacceptable. Now that it fulfils a need in our lives, it seems destined for a comeback. If you listen carefully, you'll notice that almost everyone uses this form in the spoken word, and it is reaching the point of acceptability in the written form also. In fact, during the time I was writing this book, I read that the Oxford University Press, publisher of the prestigious and well-regarded Oxford Dictionary and recognized arbiter of English usage, has now accepted this form as correct.

Second person

Writing in the second person ("you") is useful for instruction manuals, policy statements and the like. Suppose you are writing instructions for readers who are, for example, managers.

Instead of the gender specific:
Each manager is responsible for his own departmental budget.

You could say:
As manager, you are responsible for your own departmental budget.

Imperative form

Instead of the impersonal, tedious passive form:
United Way donation forms should be completed and returned to Human Resources, attention Victoria Jones.

Try:
Please return your completed United Way donation form to Victoria Jones in the Human Resources Department.

These simple methods will help make your writing gender neutral, which it must be to be effective in the business world of today.

Rule No. 5: Use correct grammar

While English spelling is a challenge to the most enthusiastic linguist, English grammar is logical. It is logical to the point that incorrect grammar can change the meaning of a sentence. For example, see if you can tell the difference *in meaning* between these two sentences:

The students, who had finished the exam, left early.
The students who had finished the exam left early.

In the first sentence, all of the students had finished the exam and all left early. In the second, only some students had finished the exam and they were the ones who left early. In the first, you can remove the phrase within the pair of commas and you will be left with the essence of the meaning: the students left early. The words within the commas provide extra information about the subject, the students. In the second case, the words *who had finished the exam* are not *extra* information, but *defining* information. They define which students we mean: those who had finished the exam.

Which of these two sentences is correct?

Mary likes John better than me.
Mary likes John better than I.

Which one did you choose? Well, you're right! Both sentences are correct, but each has a different meaning. The first means that Mary likes *John* better than she likes *me*. The second means that *Mary* likes John better than *I* like John.

Closely allied with grammar is syntax. Syntax refers to the order in which we place words in a sentence, and as the following examples show, it is often vital to meaning.

- *Lost in the dusty old files for twenty years, the lawyer discovered the contract.* ("You'll stay there until you find it!")

- *Sleeping off the effects of liquor, the policeman found two men in the corner of the deserted building.* (What happened to "Not while on duty"?)

- *A million dollars was reported stolen by bank officials.* (An inside job!)

- *The piano was sold to the lady with the Queen Ann Legs.* (She must have been a regal lady.)

- *I was referred to a doctor with acute appendicitis.* (This hurts me more than it hurts you.)

These funny examples serve to illustrate what fractured syntax does to the meaning of a sentence, but they are just funny examples. You should realize, however, that this mistake can have serious consequences. For example, a company was negotiating a new employee benefits program, and the draft contract contained this sentence:

> *By paying a premium of 5% of wages, all employees are covered under the plan.*

From this wording, who do you understand was to pay the 5% premium? According to this sentence, the employees were to pay. In fact, the intent was that the company would. The sentence should have read:

> *By paying a premium of 5% of wages, the company may cover all employees under the plan.*

This one error in syntax might easily have put the agreement in jeopardy.

So, as you can see, if you want to write well, you should pay attention to grammar. Many adults have forgotten the grammar they learned in school. If you went to school in the last twenty years or so, you may not have learned grammar at all, and are now feeling at a disadvantage. Fortunately, there is a simple answer to this problem: get a style guide. There are many on the market, some better than others, and my favourite is still the classic *Elements of Style* by Strunk and White. This small volume is constantly updated, and its reputation is such that, by quoting it as your authority, you can quell any argument about your grammar. It is now also available on line.

Rule No. 6: Use the right word in the right context

English is a rich language, which is usually a good thing. However, there is one particularly nasty little trick lying in wait for the unwary writer. It takes the form of pairs of words that look similar, and appear to have the same meanings—but they don't. Sometimes there are just shades of difference, and sometimes they mean totally different things. Business writers often confuse these words, sometimes playing havoc with what they mean to say.

Look at the following pairs of words, and see if you know the difference in meaning between the two words in each case:

1. eminent/imminent
2. complement/compliment
3. apprised/appraised
4. stationery/stationary
5. flaunt/flout
6. uninterested/disinterested
7. e.g./i.e.
8. currently/presently
9. council/counsel
10. ensure/insure

Here are the meanings, and some sentences to illustrate how the words are used.

1. A number of eminent persons attended the gala. (*eminent* means *prominent* or *powerful*)
   The Prime Minister's speech suggests an election call is imminent. (*imminent* means *about to happen*)

2. These new draperies complement the furnishings of the room. (*complement* means *go together with*)
   Thank you for your gracious compliment. (a *compliment* is a *positive comment*)

3. As a technology consultant, you should keep your clients apprised of the latest equipment. (*apprised* means *informed*)
   I must have my jewellery appraised for insurance purposes. (*appraised* means *valued*)

4. We must order more stationery. (*stationery* means *paper, envelopes, etc.*)
   The child ran out from behind a stationary vehicle. (*stationary* means *not moving*)

5. If you've got it, flaunt it! (*flaunt* means *show off*)
   A rebel is someone who flouts authority. (*flout* means *to go against*)

6. I am completely uninterested in basketball. (*uninterested* means *doesn't care*)
   The judge in a court case must be a disinterested party. (*disinterested* means *impartial*)

7. I love Italian food, e.g. pasta primavera. (*e.g.* means *for example*)
   The terms are set out in the contract we signed, i.e. the Purchase and Sale Agreement. (*i.e.* means *that is*)

8. My father is currently president of the golf club. (*currently* means *at present*)
   I'm sorry to keep you waiting, but I will be with you presently. (*presently* means *soon*)

9. The municipal council met to discuss the new by-law. (a *council* is a *committee*)
   I always appreciate your wise counsel. (*counsel* means *advice*, it can also be used as a verb meaning to *give advice* or it can also be the person giving the advice as in *legal counsel*)

10. Please ensure that the package goes out with tonight's mail. (*ensure* means *make sure*)
    You should insure your new house against fire and theft. (*insure* means *to protect* and should only be used in the sense of insurance policies)

If you use these (or other) words incorrectly in your business writing, it does terrible things to your credibility. Fortunately, there is a simple tool to correct the problem: a dictionary. Most people have a dictionary by their desks, but many of them would free a colony of moths if they were taken off the shelf because they are rarely used. Keep a dictionary near you, and use it when you are in doubt about either spelling or meaning. By the way, your computer's "spellcheck" won't help you here. It will tell you when you have made up a word that doesn't exist, but it won't tell you when you have used *imminent* when you meant *eminent*.

Rule No. 7: Write in the Active Voice

The Active Voice has nothing to do with tense. You can use the Active Voice in the past, the present or the future. The "voice" of a sentence refers to the order in which we state the three major sentence components: the subject, the verb and the object. The subject is the person or thing performing the action; the verb is the action; the object is the person or thing being acted upon.

The Active Voice places the three parts in that order, i.e. subject first, then verb, then object. For example:

> *The President* (subject) *convened* (verb) *the meeting* (object).

This order, the Active Voice, is the most natural way of expressing a thought in English. If English is your native tongue, it's the way you learned to speak it as a child. It keeps things moving forward, and 90% of the time it is the most appropriate form in business English. Unfortunately, we have reversed the ratio, and most of the time we use what we call the Passive Voice.

In the Passive Voice, we turn things around so that the object appears first, then the verb, then the subject. For example:

> *The meeting* (object) *was convened* (verb) *by the President* (subject).

The Passive Voice is not wrong. It is grammatically correct—but back to front. For this reason, it always comes across as unnatural and stilted, and therefore difficult to read. As an experiment, pull out of a file a report, memo or letter that you found particularly tedious to read, and the chances are that most of it will be in the Passive Voice.

To complicate matters, there are two versions of the Passive Voice. The one we discussed above is the Regular Passive. The second version eliminates the subject altogether, as in:

> *Your application* (object) *has been turned down* (verb).

Notice we don't say who did the turning down—it could have been anyone. That's why we call it the Divine Passive—think about it!

This is the form that is vastly overused in business correspondence. Why? One reason is that people think it sounds more businesslike. Well, it doesn't. It just sounds stuffy.

The other, probably more important, reason is that it allows us to make statements without taking responsibility for them. This sentence implies that someone other than the speaker turned the application down—

even though that may not be the case. The problem is that if you use this form over and over in a written piece, your readers will eventually catch on. Oh, they won't say to themselves, "Uh-oh, lots of Divine Passive—they must be hiding something!" It's more subliminal than that, but the repeated overuse of the Divine Passive does create discomfort in the reader's mind, thus throwing up a barrier to communication.

Is the Passive Voice ever the better choice? Yes. Use the Passive Voice when

- you don't know the subject *(The crime was committed at midnight.)*
- the action itself is more important than who is doing it *(The accused was found guilty and sentenced to five years in prison.)*

The Active Voice will inject vigour, power and forward movement into anything you write. In business, that's what you want.

Incidentally, this is another case where you can't rely on your computer. "Grammarcheck" programs will flag possible Passive constructions, but your computer can't tell the difference between a Passive (the report was *written* by me) and a straightforward past tense (I have *written* to my brother). You must learn to recognize the Passive Voice yourself and turn it around to the much more powerful Active Voice.

Rule No. 8: Avoid rambling sentences

The rambling sentence is a major barrier to communication in business writing. Why? When you, as a reader, encounter a rambling sentence in a business letter, you are forced to go back to the beginning and read it again if you want to understand it. It wanders back and forth, contains many commas and (perhaps) brackets, and often tries so hard to make a point that the meaning is completely lost. Here's an example.

> *A predominant issue, in my view, is whether our marketing information should be used to simply describe what we are and, therefore, preserve the status quo or rather, to describe where we want to be and what we want to be within the reality of who we are and thereby, hopefully, create new opportunities.*

If you find a sentence like this in your own writing, the first thing to do is see if you can easily break it into more than one sentence. Sometimes simply inserting a period will do the trick, but other times you need to reorganize the wording a little. At the same time, take the opportunity to remove any fluff or redundancy (see Rule No. 3). The following rewrite of the sentence makes the meaning clear:

> *I believe a major issue is what we want our marketing information to do. Do we want to describe who we are, and stay as we are? Alternatively, do we want to describe who we want to be, thereby possibly creating new opportunities?*

Remember, people are busy in today's business world. They want to read a piece of correspondence and understand it at once. If they have to read it twice, they often won't bother—and that's an alarming thought, when you consider how much time you spend writing. Assume you have just one shot at getting your message across, and you have a better chance at succeeding if you stay away from rambling sentences.

Rule No. 9: Be nice!

Many of the letters we send to one another in business are just not nice! We use words and phrases we would never use in conversation, and many of them create a tone we never intended.

Tone is something we relate to sound, such as the human voice. We know when someone is annoyed at us by the tone of voice they use in speaking to us. We know if they are being polite, or if they are being sarcastic. In writing, tone is just as important, but here we don't have the advantage of hearing the words spoken so they have to speak clearly on the printed page.

You must have heard the old expression, *You catch more bears with honey than you do with vinegar*. But did you ever stop to think you may be dripping vinegar in your business writing, without ever realizing it?

The following two groups of words illustrate what I mean:

Vinegar:

blame fault careless failure inferior negligence penalty complaint

Honey:

please thank you appreciate understand agree excellent service value

Just look at those vinegar words! Read them aloud and think about them for a moment. When you use these words, you automatically set up a negative environment in your reader's mind. Think, for example, about the difference in tone between these two sentences:

John did not attend the meeting.
John failed to attend the meeting.

The first one is simply a statement of fact, while the second one implies judgement. He should have been at the meeting, but he wasn't. Often we don't mean to inject that shade of meaning when we use the word *fail*, but we do.

On the other hand, consider the honey words. Your mother probably told you (mine certainly did) to say *please* and *thank you*—and it's perfectly all right to continue using them, even now that you are in the big, bad business world! When you use the honey words, you automatically set up a *positive* environment in your reader's mind, and he or she will respond accordingly.

Here is an illustration of how you can say the same thing, but with a vastly different result, by using honey words instead of vinegar.

Vinegar

> Because the *defective* motor that we purchased from you *failed to perform its function, we are dissatisfied* and are returning the *faulty* motor for *immediate replacement.*

Honey

> Although we have generally been pleased with your products, *the* on/off switch *on our new motor* does not work as it should. *We are, therefore, returning the motor and* look forward *to receiving a replacement* as soon as possible.

When you can truthfully begin by making a positive statement, then do so as I have done in this "honey" version above. Notice that the part still doesn't work, I am still returning it and I still expect it to be replaced. I'm just asking in a civilized manner.

It's worth noting that customer service people who have taken my writing seminar have told me, overwhelmingly, that they would respond more quickly, more positively and more helpfully to the second version—simply because they get so much of the first. People really don't like to be yelled at. Do you?

The problem of vinegar-laden correspondence has become more noticeable now with the advent of e-mail, and the situation is even worse here because we have a tendency to press that "send" button without carefully considering what we have written. Many a cyber-fight has started because someone unthinkingly poured vinegar into their words, when they could just as easily have smoothed the way with honey.

In editing your correspondence before it goes out, make sure you haven't inadvertently yelled at someone in writing. Try to use pleasant expressions. People are much more likely to respond as you would like if you allow them to do so with their egos intact. Be nice!

These *9 Rules* represent how I believe we can all develop good business writing habits. I suggest you incorporate them one by one into your writing every day on the job, and before long you will find writing is not the chore it perhaps once was. Even more importantly, you'll find your business writing actually communicates.

HELEN'S 9 RULES FOR BETTER BUSINESS WRITING

1. ***Write for your reader.***
2. ***Use simple words.***
3. ***Cut out the fluff.***
4. ***Use gender neutral language.***
5. ***Use correct grammar.***
6. ***Use the right word in the right context.***
7. ***Write in the Active Voice.***
8. ***Avoid rambling sentences.***
9. ***Be nice!***

Helen's 9 Rules for Pithy Presentations

We live in super-competitive times. Companies compete for business while individuals compete for jobs. Today, if you want to have career success, it's not enough just to do your job well. Today, you must be able to present well—to make the great pitch!

Why do I call it the great pitch? Because it's all selling. Whether you are actually selling a product or service, or just your ideas or ability, make no mistake, every time you stand up to make a presentation, you are selling. And those who do it well are those who succeed.

- Want to get your budget approved? Make a great pitch!
- Want employees to love your new benefits programme? Make a great pitch!
- Want to catch that great new client? Make a great pitch!

Whether it's fair or not, it's a fact that people who present well are perceived as doing everything well. So take every opportunity to present, because it's a great way to forge ahead in your career.

Unfortunately, however, many of us are afraid of presenting. We feel we don't do it well, so we see a presentation as something to be feared, rather than the opportunity to shine that it really is. If that's holding you back, *Helen's 9 Rules for Pithy Presentations* will help you. Over the course of my career I have made many presentations and watched many others present. *Helen's 9 Rules for Pithy Presentations* contain the essence of what I believe to be the most important techniques for giving effective, powerful, pithy presentations.

Rule No. 1: Set a clear objective

Everyone who attends a presentation has some idea of what he or she wants from it. You can't control other people's objectives, but you can and must be very clear about your own.

Why are you giving this presentation? ("Because my boss told me to do it" does not qualify as a reason!) What is your purpose? What is your own objective for the presentation? What do you want your audience to know, to feel, to understand, to do, at the end of it?

This question is so important, that I want you to use the following specific wording to set out your objective:

At the end of this presentation, I want.......

Write it down, and complete it. In choosing your objective, be as specific as possible. e.g. At the end of this presentation, I want the board to approve my departmental budget for next year. Notice, it is not only specific, but measurable. They will either approve it or not; I will either have achieved my objective or not. It isn't always possible to have such a measurable objective, but do make it as specific as you can.

The reason I want you to write the objective down in this form is that it will now form the "hook" on which you hang your whole presentation. This objective will be the benchmark against which you measure everything you plan to include. For that reason, I always write mine on a Post-It note and stick it on my computer monitor, where I can see it as I write. In considering each possible point I want to make, I ask myself, "Will this move me further towards my stated objective?" If the answer is yes, it goes in. If not, I must question its value.

Someone said, "If you don't know where you're going, how will you know when you are there?" Your written objective will help you recognize the finish line.

Rule No. 2: Open and close with a bang

The legal profession has brought us a principle with which we are all familiar, even though we have probably never heard of its name. It's called the Law of Primacy and Recency. Never heard of it? All it means is that people remember best what they heard first and what they heard last.

Theatre people know this law very well. Think back to a time when you went to see a musical show on stage. As you followed the crowd milling out onto the street, what tune was running through your head over and over? The big closing number of course! And that big closing number is very often a reprise of what? Right—the big opening number! Rogers & Hammerstein knew the Law of Primacy and Recency. So does Andrew Lloyd Webber. And now you do too, so how do you take advantage of this law? *Open and close with a bang.*

Let's look first at the opening.

In the first minute of your presentation, you must grab your audience. No matter whether you are addressing the whole company in an auditorium, the board of directors in the boardroom or your department at the weekly sales meeting, you must capture their attention at the start and give them a reason to listen. Contrary to popular belief among presenters, there is no such thing as a captive audience. They may have to be there in the chairs and they may not be able to walk out, but they can certainly leave mentally, and they will if you don't give them a reason to listen.

In that vital first minute or two, you must give your audience an answer to the question *What's in it for me?* Why should they listen? How can you make them want to listen?

Startling facts and provocative questions

Sometimes we are so caught up in what we want to talk about that we forget it is probably not as important to the audience as it is to us. So as soon as you stand up, hit them with a statement that makes them sit up and take notice. Your opening statement needs to tell the audience that you understand their needs and interests and are going to address them. Here's an example from one of my seminars.

Participants were departmental managers in a large law firm, including the manager of the library. His presentation dealt with his plans (or hopes!) to add space to the library, for which he needed more money in his budget. He began by telling the audience his name and position—which they already knew. Then he went on to talk about linear feet and rack shelving—ho hum! But then, buried in there among all this obscure technical talk, there was a gem: if all the lawyers were to bring their books back to the library at the same time, there would be no room for them on the shelves! Now there's a startling fact, and I recommended he use that as his opening. It is not only startling because it was probably not known to the audience, but it also paints quite a picture. I can just see all those lawyers frantically fending off falling books! By opening with that startling fact, he would have made the listeners begin to relate to the problem.

It can often be even more effective if you can start with a provocative question. A participant in another seminar was from the Information Services department of a major bank. Her department had created a program to protect the computer system against viruses, but the problem was that people didn't follow the procedure every day, as they needed to if the program was to work. Her presentation was intended to make people see the importance of the process and encourage them to do it each day. She couldn't see anything interesting enough to begin her presentation.

I asked her if she had any examples of what would happen if a virus sneaked past all these careless users. "Oh yes," she said, "last week a whole section of the hard drive "fried" because of a virus, and a department lost all its data. It was a mess." Well, I don't know about you, but I think that's pretty interesting! Her opening provocative question: "Did you know that all activity in the finance department ground to a halt last week, because a virus "fried" their section of the hard disk?" I think that would get their attention.

Speakers often use quotations from famous, or not-so-famous, people as their opening statements. If you can find one that is just right, this can be effective. It can be even more powerful if the quotation relates to something newsworthy that is happening around the time of your speech.

But whatever the source, make your opening statement give your listeners a good reason to pay attention to you.

Memorize the first two minutes

I don't recommend that you write your presentation out like a speech, and we'll discuss the reasons for that a little later. However, there are two exceptions: the opening and the close. Once you have decided on the statement or question that will grab your listeners, follow this three-step process:

1. Write it out
2. Translate it
3. Memorize it.

Carefully write out not only your provocative question or startling fact, but also what you plan to say immediately afterwards. Write out what you will say to introduce the main content of your presentation. That's step 1. Step 2: Translate it from the written form to the spoken form. For example, when we write we usually use words and phrases like *cannot, will not, there is*. But when we speak, we're more likely to say *can't, won't* and *there's*. So go through your opening and convert it to the spoken word—read it aloud when you have finished to make sure it sounds natural. Then go to step 3, and memorize the first two minutes of your presentation.

The main reason for memorizing your opening is that you will then be able to look your audience in their collective eye as you speak. This is your first opportunity to connect with your audience, but you won't do that if you are looking down to read from your notes. We'll be looking later at the importance of eye contact throughout your presentation, but nowhere is it more important than in the opening. So memorize the first two minutes, look at your audience, smile and begin.

We'll talk about the body of your material later, but for now let's skip to your big close.

When deciding what to say to close your presentation, refer once again to that little note you made to yourself at the beginning—your objective. "At the end of this presentation, I want....". Whatever you say at the end should speak directly to that objective. If your objective was to have the Board approve your budget—ask them for approval. If you said you wanted the prospective client to sign a contract—metaphorically hand them the pen with your closing statement. In other words, follow the time-honoured sales principle: to close the sale, ask for the order.

But your close is more than just a sentence. You must somehow encapsulate your entire message in those last few precious moments, so how can you do that? Let's look at a few effective types of close.

Review your major points

This does not, of course, mean saying it all over again. It means summarizing your points succinctly to reinforce the message in your audience's minds. At the end of all my *Helen's 9 Rules* presentations, for example, I put up a slide listing all nine rules. I don't read it aloud, nor do I talk about any one of them. Instead, I leave it up while I talk to the audience about how I want them to use the rules to improve their business lives. In your case, you might want to list the topics aloud, or even summarize the whole presentation in a few well chosen words.

Tell them what you want them to do

This is the classic "close the sale, ask for the order" close.

Have you ever received a subscription solicitation from a magazine? Mail order masters use this technique to perfection. The last item on the sales letter is what they call the "call to action". In other words, they tell you what they want you to do: "Don't be disappointed—send in your order today!" The reason they always do this is simple: it works. Tell people what you want them to do, and chances are they'll do it.

Refer to your opening

"As I said at the beginning..." is a phrase that reminds your audience of the reason you gave them for listening to you. A great opening can lead directly to a great close, and if the body of your presentation has lived up to your audience's needs, your objective will be met.

Close with a great quote

Whatever your topic, whatever your opinion, whatever you are selling, you can be sure there's a quotation somewhere that speaks directly to it, and with impact. Quotes can be effective anywhere in your presentation, if they emphasize a point you are making. At the end, though, they have added value if they hit the nail exactly on the head. The business section of your bookstore probably has at least a dozen books of quotations, and there are huge collections of quotes on the Internet. Find the section that deals with your topic, and choose a great one. Then build up to it with references to your presentation before delivering the quote with just the right degree of appropriate emotion. It works every time!

Once you have decided how to close your presentation, do the same as you did with your opening:

1. Write out your closing statement
2. Translate it
3. Memorize it.

The reasons are the same as with the opening, but with a couple more.

First, if you find you are running out of time, you can quickly jump to your memorized close. Your audience will never know anything was missed if you do it smoothly enough and with confidence.

Even more importantly, by memorizing the close you give yourself the opportunity to address your audience directly, with no distractions. Switch off your projector or computer. If you are on a platform, you might be able to step down and walk towards the audience. If the setting is a conference room, step away from your speaking position and your visual aids equipment, and address the audience face-to-face from a different perspective. This clearly gives a signal that you are about to finish, which automatically makes people pay attention.

And remember those crowds humming the big closing number as they leave the theatre. Make sure they are singing ***your*** song as they leave the meeting.

Rule No. 3: Break your talk into bite-sized pieces

Inexperienced presenters are often overwhelmed by the sheer volume of what they think they have to say on a topic. They feel they must tell their audience everything they know. If you do that, your audience will be overwhelmed too!

It's a matter of deciding how much of what you know needs to be in the presentation, and what can either be forgotten or at least kept in reserve for the question and answer period. Once again, refer to your stated objective. For each piece of information you think of including, ask yourself "Will this move me towards my stated objective?" If not—out it goes.

Once you have a handle on what you do want to include, it probably still looks like a lot of information. To make it easier for you to compile your presentation, and easier for your audience to absorb it, break it into bite-sized pieces. Jot your notes for each "bite" on a separate sheet of paper—I find this another use for the invaluable Post-It note. The next task is to divide them up according to the shape you decide to give your presentation. There are a number of useful formulas that can help you put your presentation in order, and you will choose different formulas at different times, depending on the subject and the objective of your presentation. Here are just a few.

Chronological

This is probably the least interesting formula to work with, but often appropriate. If you are an accountant, for example, presenting the case for taking a business public, you might want to tell the company's story from its humble beginnings to its present stage. This sets the stage for your proposal, giving you the opportunity to project the story into the best possible future.

Problem/solution

Have you ever seen those sets of "before and after" photos that diet product makers use to advertise their wares? The "before" photograph always shows the person in the worst possible light—facing directly at the camera, sloppy clothes, unkempt hair and generally looking terrible. That makes the "after" version even more attractive. It's a legitimate marketing ploy, and one you can use effectively in your presentation.

Identify a situation that your audience will recognize as a problem. Then describe it in terms that point out exactly the breadth and depth of the difficulty. Then dazzle them with your solution!

Old way/new way

As its name suggests, this is a good formula to use when introducing a new method of doing something, a new process or even a new product. Again, take every opportunity to highlight the ways in which the new way is an improvement on the old.

Goal/roadmap

This is effective only if you have a goal that the audience will accept. Larger market share, leadership of the industry, global presence, a cure for a deadly disease are all goals that lend themselves to this formula. Now you need only describe "how we can get there from here'.

Objections/answers

If you are trying to sell an idea, a product or a service to an audience you know well, this can be effective. Simply think of all the objections they are likely to raise, and counter them methodically throughout your presentation. If they have no objections left to raise, you have a good chance of attaining your objective.

Topical

This is the route to take when you have a number of seemingly unrelated topics, joined only by means of your presentation. You must put them in the order you think most useful and find appropriate ways of leading from one to the other. *Helen’s 9 Rules* is one example of a topical formula.

Now that you have your information organized, and you know what you want to say, you might wonder how you are going to remember it all. **Don’t write it out like a speech**. If you do that, you *will* read it, no matter how hard you try not to. Then if you lose your place, you’ll have no way of getting back on track until you find it—that way lies panic.

Instead of writing it out, use “cheatsheets”. Cheatsheets are a time-honoured way for speakers to keep on track in a presentation, avoid forgetting what to say and keep the presentation sounding natural. You’ll be able to maintain eye contact with your audience, and there will be less chance of losing your place.

Cheatsheets can take several forms, depending on the situation and your own preference.

Index cards are useful for speeches which are not supported by visual aids. Simply hold them in your hand in a natural way and glance at each one as you begin the topic. You don't need to hide them—nobody minds your using memory aids, so long as you don't focus on them instead of the audience. The secret to good index cards is to put only a few key words on them—not whole sentences and certainly not paragraphs. Use a heavy black marker so that you can easily read the words. Of course, you must know your subject well enough to be able to pick up on the key words and speak to them fluently.

If your presentation is a long one—such as a seminar—and particularly if you must give the same one many times, a three-ring binder is a good choice. The principle is the same as index cards, but you can put a little more on each sheet in your binder. Perhaps use one sheet for notes on each overhead transparency. Again, use as few words as practical and write in bold letters so that you can read them at a glance.

If you use overheads, put them either in cardboard frames or clear plastic flipframes. Then you can print large key words on the frames, where only you can see them. This creates a good impression with the audience, because it's not apparent that you are using notes at all. Of course, this method does tie you fairly closely to the projector, but if you practise you can learn to take the notes in at a glance as you place the overhead on the glass.

If you know your subject well, the overheads or slides themselves can often act as built-in cheatsheets. Simply glance at the visual and the words will tell you what you want to talk about and what to say. This is my own preferred method, and the most audience-friendly way of remembering material. Remember, though, the key is to know your material very well.

The effective use of cheatsheets can help you establish rapport with your audience and a professional aura about yourself as a presenter.

Rule No 4: Make your visuals aid

Here's a common scenario among less successful business presenters.

The company comptroller must make a financial presentation to the Board of Directors. Since she dreads the event so much, she leaves it until the last minute before she begins to prepare the presentation. At the "eleventh hour", she finally dictates her speech and has it typed up in large letters, double spaced. If there are six people expected at the meeting, she makes six copies and then, almost as an afterthought, one extra on overhead transparencies. The pages of this last copy then become her visual aids!

We've all sat through these presentations, haven't we? The presenter puts up a slide completely full of words in one or two paragraphs. Often we can't read it, but that doesn't matter because the speaker then turns around, addresses the screen and reads it for us. Then, just in case we miss a word we can refer to our handouts—which are an exact copy—and read it ourselves! You have to ask yourself why the presentation is needed at all. A memo would have accomplished the same objective.

Because of the nature of her information, our comptroller makes the other classic visual aid mistake: she puts up transparencies of large, complicated financial statements. When you do that, you can be absolutely guaranteed that at no point will the attention of all your audience members be focused exactly where you want it to be. There's simply too much for them to try to take in—and of course they are no longer listening to you. This is a control issue. It's your presentation and you need to make sure the audience's attention is with you all the way. Don't lose them because they are wading through masses of data on your slides.

If you want to show financial information, it's best done with graphic devices such as charts and graphs. Here are a few possibilities.

A Comparisons between sums of money, such as this year vs last year or actual vs budget, can be shown by bar charts. Sums of money are typically shown as vertical columns, while lengths of time are usually horizontal bars. Generally, avoid 3D bars, as they can be confusing. Flat ones in contrasting colours work well.

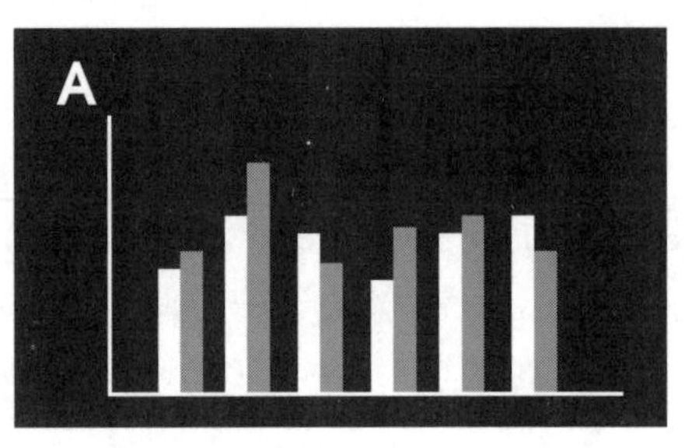

B The relationship of parts to a whole, such as product or service mix, jumps right off the screen when you show them as a pie chart. You can add to the effect by "exploding" pie charts, where individual slices seem to separate from the whole pie. Don't get carried away with special effects though—remember, the data is the important thing.

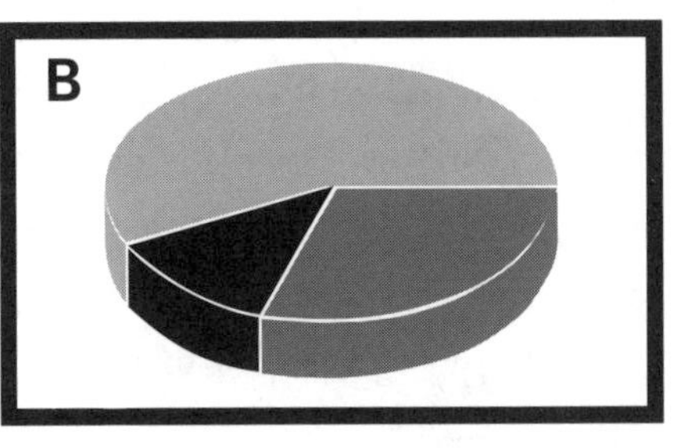

C Trends are clear when shown as graphs. You can even show a number of trends on the same graph by using different coloured lines or dotted/dashed lines. Don't use too many figures, as they make your graphs too cluttered and hard to read.

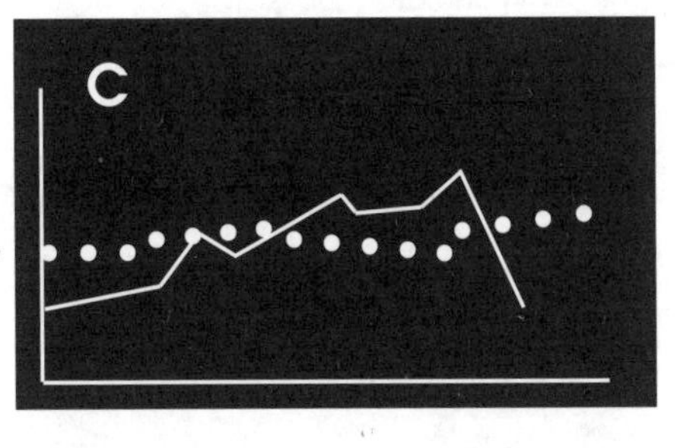

D For information that doesn't lend itself to graphic representation, use words. But instead of large blocks of text, use *word charts*. These are series of bullet points made up of phrases rather than sentences. Say just enough to highlight what you will talk about, so that people will glance at the screen and then bring their attention back to you.

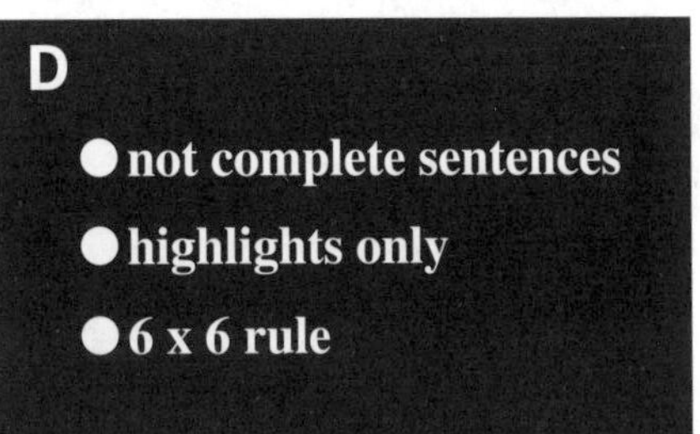

A great source of frustration to audiences is the use of letters and figures that are too small to read. Use the space on the screen. Here's a simple tip to find out if your letters are big enough. Type up the transparency and place it on the floor at your feet. If you can read the type from a standing position, it will be legible when projected. If you are using 35mm slides, hold the slide up to the light at arm's length. If you can read it, so will your audience.

To help you make the most of word charts, follow the "6 x 6" guideline: no more than six words to a line, no more than six lines to a frame. If you keep it roughly to this count and take the arm's length test, your audience will be able to read your visual aids comfortably.

Remember, they are called visual aids for good reason. They are supposed to aid you in getting your message across. They should therefore support your speech, not take its place.

It's important to be able to sharply focus your audience's attention where you want it at any time. I've found the best tool for this purpose is a laser pointer. It's small enough to fit in your hand when not in use, and its sharp, bright red presence draws everyone's eyes wherever it goes on the screen. Buy a good quality laser pointer, and make sure it always has fresh batteries.

Rule No. 5: Hand out the right things at the right time

Poorly timed handouts can be a presentation killer.

Suppose you are making a financial presentation to top executives. Before you start, you hand each person a thick sheaf of financial statements. Naturally, the executives are vitally interested in this information, so what do you think they do? You guessed it—they begin to read the financials and forget all about you. Once again, you have lost control of your presentation by failing to keep your audience's attention on what you are saying.

Hand out materials at the last possible moment before you refer to them. In this example, you would serve yourself much better by telling the executives you will be giving them a complete set of financials at the end of your presentation. In the meantime, use your carefully crafted visual aids to focus their attention on the points you want to make about the financial situation. This way the audience has the comfort of knowing in-depth information will be available later, and you have control over the presentation. Everybody wins.

Remember, you are the main component of the presentation. The information you put up on your visual aids should be a brief focus point for what you are saying, and the handouts should contain more detailed information for your audience's later reference. As a general rule, let your visuals show less than you say, and your handouts much more. This method ensures that each component plays its part and supports the other two, for the best possible transfer of information.

Rule No. 6: Finish on time

Nobody minds if you finish a little early—but people hate it when you run over your time. This is especially true if others are also scheduled to present after you, but you should bear it in mind even when you are the only speaker.

Plan your presentation to finish five minutes early. It's also a good assumption that you will begin five minutes late, so build these two margins into your timing plan. "Timing plan?", I hear you ask. Yes. A successful presentation must be carefully timed, or you run the risk of rambling, running overtime and possibly not having time for your big finish. An otherwise effective presentation will be ruined if you have to just fade out instead of bringing it to its proper close.

Given your total speaking time, and knowing the number of bite-sized pieces you want to include, you must now decide how much time to allot to each. The next job is to make up a timing sheet, showing each module, how long it will take and when it will finish. To illustrate this, I'll use *Helen's 9 Rules for Pithy Presentations* and assume the presentation is scheduled to begin at noon and run for one hour. My timing sheet would look like the figure opposite.

Timing for Pithy Presentations, 1 hour version, start at noon	
	Finish at
Intro (start 12.05, take 2 minutes)	12.07
Rule 1: Set a clear objective (3 min.)	12.10
Rule 2: Open and close with bang (10 min.)	12.20
Rule 3: Bite sized pieces (7 minutes)	12.27
Rule 4: Make visuals aid (9 min.)	12.36
Rule 5: Hand out right things at right time (2 min.)	12.38
Rule 6: Finish on time (3 min.)	12.41
Rule 7: Connect with audience (5 min)	12.46
Rule 8: Tame the butterflies (5 min.)	12.51
Rule 9: Rehearse (2 min.)	12.53
Close: (2 minutes)	12.55

I also have a further breakdown of the rules, so that I can make adjustments if I find I am running late or early. There are certain stories or examples I can take out if I am late, and others I have on hand to insert if I have run ahead of time.

Besides this sheet, there are two more items you will need to keep you on schedule.

- First, your cheatsheets. Whether your notes are on index cards, sheets in a ring binder or the frames of your slides, you should make a note on each one of the time you expect to finish that point or section of your presentation. Use a thick marker or red ink, so that you can see it easily at a glance.

- The other essential item is a clock you can put in front of you, or near the projector, where you can see it at all times. Don't count on there being a clock in the room where you will present, because even if there is, it may not be in a place where you can easily see it. Bring your own. I have a smart little brass clock that usually stands on my desk, except when I am presenting—then it's right in front of me. A small travel alarm is also good. Caution: don't use your wristwatch for this purpose. If you keep glancing at your watch, you will give the audience the impression you would rather be somewhere else. A few years ago during an election campaign, then U.S. President Bush appeared in a televised "town hall" debate. He kept glancing at his watch, no doubt purely to see how he could make the best use of the time available. Unfortunately for him, many television viewers saw it as a sign that he wasn't interested in the proceedings, and it certainly cost him some support—perhaps even votes.

Each time you finish a point or a module of your presentation, you glance either at the note on your cheatsheet or on your timing sheet and compare that time to what the clock shows. You can tell immediately whether you are on time at any given point in your program.

Audiences always appreciate a speaker who finishes on time.

Rule No. 7: Connect with your audience

People often ask me how to create rapport with their audiences. The way to do that is to make a connection, so that each person feels individually included in the presentation. If you think of your presentation not as a speech, but as a conversation with the audience, you will be more likely to include everyone, and your delivery will be more natural.

Here are some guidelines to help you connect with your audience.

Eye Contact

Have you ever had a conversation with someone who looked at a point behind your left ear instead of at you? How did that make you feel? You probably had the impression either that you couldn't trust the other person, or at the very least that he or she wasn't very interested in the conversation. Now think of someone you know who, when you talk, always makes you feel important and interesting. Chances are that person looks you right in the eye as you speak.

You can take this knowledge with you as you step up to present. The first thing you do is consciously make eye contact with people in the audience. If you are addressing a small number of people around a table, it is relatively easy to include everyone. When you address a large group in an auditorium, it's a little more of a challenge. You can't possibly ensure you meet the eye of everyone in a 200-person audience, but you can make them feel as if you have. How? Simply look directly at a small number of faces, say three, in one part of the room. Then move your eyes slowly to a point somewhere else in the room and take in three people there. If you let your eyes rove over the audience in this way throughout your presentation, everyone in the room will feel included.

Expression

Smile. A deadpan expression is boring and offputting. Most of us smile less than we realize, with the result that we don't make the most of this marvellous facial expression that can make the difference between a positive and a negative impression. Practise smiling at yourself in the mirror. Notice how you look when you smile. Even more important, notice how your facial muscles feel so that you will be aware of when you are smiling and when you are not.

Use facial expression to add to the impact of your words. Let your face reflect enthusiasm, happiness, sadness, humour as appropriate throughout your presentation.

Pay attention also to the expression in your voice. Vary the pace and pitch of your voice to mirror your words. If you open by saying how happy you are to be there, but your face doesn't smile, your voice is monotone and you don't look at your audience—do you think they will believe you?

Body Language

When we interact with others, we say much more than we think before we even open our mouths. We give messages through the use of body language.

This is a very broad subject, and it's not the purpose of this book to study it in detail. What I do want to do, however, is show you how to take advantage of body language to give your presentations more impact.

When people find out I speak about presentation skills, usually the first question they ask is, "What do I do with my hands?" It's as if we never had hands before, until we had to make a presentation and then suddenly there they were—two foreign objects at the ends of our arms! What should we do with them? The answer is simple: use them as you normally use them.

There are a few things you should **not** do with your hands:

- Don't shove them down into your pockets because you will pull your clothing out of shape and look sloppy.
- Don't clasp them together behind your back. That creates an impression that you have something to hide.
- Don't clasp them in front of you in the "fig leaf" position, which tends to make you look as if you are addressing a group of small children rather than adults at a business presentation.

Use your hands and arms in wide, sweeping gestures that bring your audience into the zone of your speech. You'll find this action also helps make you comfortable and reduces nerves. As with any technique, of course, don't overdo this or it can become distracting.

Stand tall. Pull yourself up to your full height and project your voice with confidence.

If you are on a platform, or even if you have lots of room around the boardroom table, use the space. Move around and address your audience from slightly different perspectives. This also increases their feeling of connection with you. Move slowly and deliberately, however, as short, quick movements can be unnerving for your audience.

Above all, remember that when there is conflict between your words and your body language, people will believe your non-verbal message. Work in front of a mirror, or better still videotape yourself as you speak, and carefully study your body language. It's one area where a little work can pay big dividends.

Names

It's been said that the sweetest sound in the world to a person is the sound of his or her own name. You will deepen the connection with your audience if you address them by name whenever possible. For small internal presentations, you may well know the individuals by name and this makes your job easier. At larger gatherings, people often wear name tags—take advantage of them during your speech. People will be delighted to be personally addressed.

It's also important to pronounce names correctly. If someone's name is a little difficult for you, try to pronounce it and ask if you are right. Most people will be pleased to help, and flattered that you made the attempt. Remember, the correct way to pronounce someone's name is the way that person wants it pronounced. If, for example, someone has a name that is obviously Italian or French, but they pronounce it according to English sounds, then that is the correct way *for that person*. If you insist on pronouncing it "correctly", you will antagonize the person and look foolish at the same time. So take your pronunciation cue from the owner of the name.

If you remember that your audience is made up of individuals, and present as if you were speaking to each one in turn, you will achieve a connection with your audience that greatly improves your chances of presentation success.

Rule No. 8: Tame the butterflies

According to many studies, public speaking is the number one fear in society today—even before fear of death! I have no magic pill to take away presentation stress, but I do have some thoughts that might help you control it.

First, recognize that what you feel just before you make a presentation is just stagefright, and everyone gets it. Steps you can take to feel more comfortable encompass both physical remedies and mental remedies.

Physical Remedies

The simplest thing you can do is to practise deep breathing before you begin. The type of breathing taught in yoga works well. For this, you first breathe in slowly through your nose for a count of four, hold for four and then exhale through your mouth for a count of eight. This can be done quite surreptitiously even in the meeting room just before you stand up to speak.

The next two are definitely to be done *before* you enter the presentation room. Remember when you were a child you used to hold contests with your friends to see who could make the funniest face? Try it again, in front of a mirror. Stretch your face every which way, as far as you can. The muscles you are flexing are the ones you use to speak, so you will loosen them up and make it easier to speak naturally. As a bonus, you will make yourself laugh, which automatically eases tension.

Take a pencil and put it in your mouth crosswise, like a horse's bit. Repeat a tongue-twister three times: something like "she sells seashells on the seashore". Then take the pencil out and repeat it three more times. Once again, you have exercised your speaking muscles. If you are one of the many who fear your mouth will freeze up and you won't be able to utter a word, this one is for you.

Just before you rise to speak, press the nail of your first finger into the flesh of your thumb until it stings a little. Your senses will focus on this slight discomfort, and you will forget the fluttering in your tummy. Once you begin speaking, you will automatically release the pressure on your fingers as you concentrate on your presentation.

Mental Remedies

We've all heard how successful athletes visualize themselves at the finish line, arms raised in ecstatic triumph as they win the race. They do it because it works. This practical exercise is available to you too. Before the presentation, close your eyes and relax. See yourself standing up, comfortably going through your presentation. Finally, see the president shaking your hand, congratulating you on your success. You'll be surprised how often it unfolds exactly as you visualized.

Closely linked to visualization is the practice of affirmation. This entails composing strong, positive statements about your presentation and repeating them to yourself continually until they are ingrained in your consciousness. Let me share one of my own success affirmations. Each time I arrive at a client's office to facilitate a workshop, as I go up in the elevator I repeat to myself, "This is going to be great. I'm going to enjoy it, they're going to enjoy it, they're going to learn and the client is going to get its moneysworth!" It settles my mind and prepares me to go in and do the best workshop I can.

The term "stagefright" is a misnomer because you don't feel it when you are on stage. You feel it while waiting in the wings to go on stage. Once you start the performance, it goes away—and the same thing happens to presentation nerves.

It's also worth noting that the best actors would not want to be without their stagefright. Sir Laurence Olivier once said, "The day I lose my stagefright is the day I will stop acting." Actors use the adrenalin rush to take their performances to a higher level. So don't worry about those butterflies—let your presentation soar on their wings!

Rule No. 9: Rehearse! Rehearse! Rehearse!

Everyone pays lip service to this rule, but expert presenters do much more than that. If you don't rehearse properly, your performance will suffer.

A proper rehearsal involves making the complete presentation out loud, not just going over small parts of it in your mind.

If you don't do the whole thing, how will you know how long it will take? In order to pace the presentation and make use of the timing techniques mentioned in *Rule No. 6, Finish on Time*, you must know exactly how much time is taken up with each section of your speech. Use a stopwatch to time yourself as you make the presentation, repeating the most important points until you are sure of the wording and the timing. Then you can complete your timing sheet.

Your rehearsal should take place in as close to the presentation conditions as possible. If you are to present in the boardroom, stay late in the office one evening. When everyone else has left, go into the boardroom and make the presentation. That way you can get a feel for the room itself, and even work with the equipment if it is already in place. Of course, it's important to work with the equipment to make sure you can incorporate your visual aids fluently into the presentation.

If you can't do this, try to do your rehearsal for an audience, even if only one person. When I began speaking professionally, I asked my husband to watch my first rehearsal. I wasn't one minute into the speech when he asked me, "Why are you swaying? You'll make them all seasick if you do that!" I hadn't realized I was swaying from side to side, and would probably have continued to distract my audience with this habit if I hadn't rehearsed in front of someone. So choose someone you can trust, and listen carefully to their reaction to your presentation.

If all else fails, do your presentation in front of a full-length mirror. Pay attention to your expression, body language and movements. You may even catch yourself in an unconscious mannerism that could be distracting to your audience.

Remember, a presentation is a performance. Rehearsal is vital to its success.

So there you have *Helen's 9 Rules for Pithy Presentations*. The need for persuasive presentation skills isn't new. In ancient times, the Greek philosopher and educator Pericles said, "The thinking human being not able to express himself stands at the same level as those who cannot think." Think about that. What he's saying is that you might be smart, but if you can't express youself well you might as well not be. Do you take every opportunity to present your ideas to those who can make a difference? You must. To succeed, you must be able to express those ideas logically, cohesively and powerfully. In other words, you must make the great pitch.

Learn to shape your ideas into logical presentations, illustrate them with strong visual aids and present them with panache. Take every opportunity to present: to your peers, to management, to clients, to the little league, to anyone who'll listen. Because the more you present, the better you'll present.

So go out there now, and pitch your way to success!

Helen's 9 rules for Pithy Presentations

1. *Set a clear objective.*
2. *Open and close with a bang.*
3. *Break your talk into bite-sized pieces.*
4. *Make your visuals aid.*
5. *Hand out the right things at the right time.*
6. *Finish on time.*
7. *Connect with your audience.*
8. *Tame the butterflies.*
9. *Rehearse! Rehearse! Rehearse!*

Helen's 9 Rules for Lively Listening

Poor listening habits are the cause of more communication breakdown than most of us realize, mainly because we don't think of listening as a communication skill. But it is. The first thing to realize about listening is what it's not. It's not the same as hearing and it's not waiting for your turn to speak

Hearing involves only the mechanism inside your ears. Sound waves reverberate off your eardrum, producing words you can recognize, as well as other sounds you must interpret. It happens all the time, even with sounds of which you are not consciously aware: traffic in the street, radio or television playing in the background, the conversation at the next table in the restaurant. But that's not listening (although I must admit, I sometimes do listen to the group at the next table!).

When someone else is speaking, you usually are not. Usually, there will be silence from your side of the conversation. But if you are running over your reply in your mind and just waiting until the other person finishes so that you can jump in, that's not listening.

Listening is a conscious act, and if we don't practise it actively and carefully, we simply cannot communicate effectively and fully. That's what this section is all about. So let's consider *Helen's 9 Rules for Lively Listening*.

Rule No. 1: Decide to listen

No wonder we shut out a great deal of noise around us today—there's so much of it. If we actually listened to everything, we would soon go into overload and run screaming into the sunset, never to be seen again! So we have done what human beings always do: we've adapted. We now have a built-in filter that lets us shut out all the extraneous noise that doesn't interest us, so that we can concentrate on what does. The problem is that we often rely too heavily on the mechanism, and end up filtering out messages we need to hear.

In business settings, we can't afford to let that happen, so we must actually *decide* to listen and then do it actively, with concentration and intent, using all the skills we'll be discussing in this section.

Why should we listen? Here are just a few reasons:

Listening keeps us informed

A common cry in business today is, "Nobody ever tells me anything around here!" It's usually heard when someone has just found out something he or she should have known before, and this exclamation tries to lay the blame on someone else for that lack of knowledge. How often, on the other hand, have you ever heard someone say, "I never listen around here"? Make a point of paying attention to what's going on around you, of listening to information and messages from your colleagues, so that you will always be well informed. According to current wisdom, knowledge is power. The easiest way to acquire knowledge is to listen.

Listening keeps us out of trouble.

Perhaps you remember your mother, when you were quite young, saying something like, "I've told you over and over not to do that. Don't you listen?" The answer, of course, is that we didn't. We didn't realize it at the time, but we always had more interesting things on our minds than instructions from Mom so the information did, as my own mother used to say, go in one ear and out the other!

Unfortunately, this situation isn't confined to children. Many of us carry poor listening habits over to the grown-up business world. If someone is giving you instructions and you don't listen properly, there's a good chance you won't be able to carry them out well. Over time, this can be detrimental to your career.

Listening makes us appreciated.

One of my best friends in university, Eleanore, was very popular. More than once I heard someone say, "When you are with Eleanore she makes you feel you are the most important person in the world." The reason for that was that Eleanore was a great listener. She listened with her ears, her eyes, her smile, her body, her mind—her whole self. When you put that much of yourself into the listening end of a conversation, the other person can't help admiring and appreciating you.

In business, the good listeners will often find themselves chosen for the most coveted projects simply because other people enjoy working with them.

Rule No. 2: Avoid selective listening

Mary had just finished a job interview, and the interviewer said, "You seem well qualified for the job and I like your attitude. I'll get back to you when I have interviewed the other ten candidates." She was quite surprised when she didn't get the job. Why? Because she listened only to what she wanted to hear, and conveniently (or inconveniently, as it turned out!) ignored mention of the stiff competition.

In business as in life, we can't afford to practise selective listening. The fact that we ignore the bad news doesn't make it go away! In fact, things might well become worse if we act on just one part of a complex message.

One way we listen selectively is not listening to the end of what the other person is saying. Someone says half a sentence and we immediately leap to the end, assuming we know what they were about to say and so we don't listen to the rest. Has anyone ever done this when you were speaking? Then you know how annoying it is! The words, "That's not what I was going to say" are like a dash of cold water in our faces—and we deserve it.

A common cause of selective listening is personal bias against the speaker. I attended a board meeting at which representatives of an advertising agency were presenting their proposal for an ad campaign to a national association. I overheard one man say to his neighbour, "You can't trust a word these ad boys say." Obviously, someone with this attitude is not going to listen to the presentation with an open mind, and in fact may not listen at all. That's selective listening.

It's also tempting to discount the opinions of people you simply don't like. If you feel yourself mentally switch off when a certain person begins to speak, you are guilty of selective listening. Remember, the information may be valid and useful even if the person delivering it is never going to be on your Christmas card list—so listen up!

Rule No. 3: Give acknowledgement and feedback

You can acknowledge what someone is saying through a verbal or non-verbal response. A simple nod of the head, a smile, a raising of the eyebrows: these are all forms of non-verbal acknowledgement. They let the speaker know you are paying attention.

If you prefer to acknowledge verbally, you might inject into the conversation such phrases as: *I understand...Really?... I didn't know that.* Notice, this indicates your understanding, not necessarily your agreement. If you don't agree, your chance to express your concerns will come later.

These forms of acknowledgement give the speaker comfort in knowing that you are understanding what is being said. They demonstrate your interest and deepen the rapport between you. It was in this area that my friend Eleanore excelled, and that's how she made people feel so important.

In a meaningful conversation, each party acknowledges the other's *feelings* as well as the actual words that are spoken. For example, suppose a co-worker is complaining bitterly to you about a seemingly trivial matter. Joanna frowns and angrily exclaims, "Why don't they print these meeting announcements on coloured paper or something? How do they expect me to pay attention to yet another piece of white paper that gets lost among everything else on this desk?" You could, of course, simply agree that it's an interesting idea, or you could say you don't have a problem with the white paper—but in either case you might well be missing the point. If, on the other hand, you respond to Joanna's feelings and say, "This really seems to have you upset", you open up the possibility for her to explore the reason for this. Before long, it becomes apparent that Joanna is feeling overwhelmed by her workload, and the announcement buried on the papers on her desk is just the last straw. Effective listening provides a positive contribution to the discussion.

It is worth noting here that men and women react differently to this type of acknowledgement. As a rule, men are reluctant to discuss their feelings, and are quite likely to deny them. When responding to a man in this situation, make sure you preface with an exploratory phrase such as *it seems to me*, *could it be*, or *I wonder if*. Women tend to be more open to comment on their feelings, although you still need to proceed with some sensitivity.

It's important to watch the language you use in giving feedback. If you use phrases such as *my advice is*, *your problem is* or *what you should do*, you may think this is positive feedback. However, it may not be welcome. If you give the speaker an opportunity to talk the problem through, he or she will often come up with the answer, which is much more effective. Sometimes a well-meaning listener may downplay a problem with a response like *don't worry*, or *that's not so bad*. Again, this may seem like encouragement, but it can actually be perceived as devaluing the person's concern. It is a well known fact in the nursing world that seriously ill patients are often frustrated by people's unwillingness to acknowledge their situation. It doesn't help a terminally ill person for a visitor to say brightly, "Don't worry—you'll be better in no time and winning the ski championship again this winter!", when the patient knows perfectly well that he or she is unlikely to be well again. This is a situation where an effective listener would offer evidence of understanding, rather than trite assurances.

Reflective Listening

Reflective listening is a form of acknowledgement and feedback that is open to some misunderstanding and misuse. As the name suggests, it simply means taking the message the speaker is sending and returning it to the speaker for confirmation. However, reflecting is not the same as parroting! Before sending the message back, you need to *rephrase* it. Consider, for example, the following:

Richard: I'm fed up writing draft reports for Tom to take to the meetings and then never hearing whether they went anywhere or not.

Jerry: So what you're saying is that you're fed up writing draft reports for Tom to take to the meetings and then never hearing whether they went anywhere or not. Is that right?

That's pretty silly, isn't it? That's parroting. Putting it in the form of reflective listening would result in something like this:

Richard: I'm fed up writing draft reports for Tom to take to the meetings and then never hearing whether they went anywhere or not.

Jerry: It sounds as if you are frustrated by not receiving feedback from Tom about your reports. Is that right?

That's reflective listening. It's not always appropriate to do this, but it can be a very useful method of making sure, for example, that you have instructions correct before acting on them.

Rule No. 4: Ask appropriate questions

You may wonder why the act of asking questions is included in what I call "lively listening". The reason is that my understanding of the listening process includes helping the other party to convey his or her thoughts. By asking the right questions, you can greatly affect the breadth and depth of the conversation That is the real art of listening. Here's how effective questioning works.

1) Social worker: Has Johnny been in school every day this week?

2) Social worker: How is Johnny doing in school now that we've got him into the Special Education program?

These examples illustrate two major types of question: closed and open.

The first example is a closed question, which means it can be answered by a simple *yes* or *no*. The second is an open question, because the other person must elaborate and give information in order to answer it. You can't answer an open question with *yes* or *no*. Both types of questions have their uses.

If you want to develop and broaden a conversation, start by asking open ended questions. Then, as the need for confirmation arises, insert closed ended questions where appropriate. Continuing the example:

Social worker: How is Johnny doing in school now that we've got him into the Special Education program?

Mother: OK

Social worker: How do you think his behaviour has changed?

Mother: He's not as difficult at home.

Social worker: What do you mean by that?

Mother: Well, he used to come home from his old school with a "mad" face on, throw his stuff down and never speak to me or his brother. Now he yells, "Hi Mom, I'm home!" on his way to the fridge.

Social worker: And you attribute the change to the program?

Mother: Yes.

Social worker: What else do you think Johnny needs now?

Mother: Well, I think your visits help.

Social worker: So you don't want me to stop calling on him just yet?

Mother: No. Can we give it at least another month?

You can use both types of questions to broaden a conversation, confirm or clarify meaning and then move the conversation in another direction. Here are examples of how you use questions for these purposes.

Broadening

- Mary, you've told us about the new procedure they are using in the Toronto branch and it seems to be working well. How do you think we can adapt it to suit our conditions in Montreal?
- We've agreed that we have a major problem competing against the established brand in the marketplace. Does anyone have any ideas as to how we can make people notice our house brand?

Note: These questions call for an analytic response that will bring in more information and broaden the discussion.

Clarifying or confirming

- What do you mean?
- Are you saying you agree with Doug's assessment?
- So, you think we can achieve our sales target for this quarter?

Note: By asking these questions, you give the speaker an opportunity to restate a position and clarify it for the other parties.

Changing direction

- We've discussed your proposed program in depth and it seems to have merit. Can you tell us what impact it will have on the budget?
- OK. I see how a marketing blitz would help us raise awareness of the product line. But how can we do this with the small number of sales reps we have?

Note: These questions bring closure to one part of the discussion and move it on to another aspect.

Do you see how the open ended questions elicit information, and the closed ended ones serve to confirm information or opinion? Think about your own conversations. Do you use questions effectively? Questioning is a valid and helpful aspect of listening, so it's important to work on it.

Rule No 5: Listen for non-verbal cues

Suppose for a moment that you live in a different place from the one where you grew up, and you have gone "home" on vacation. For the first week you have spent every day and evening with your mother, and you have thoroughly enjoyed her company. Now, an old friend has invited you out for dinner. As you leave, you say, "OK Mom, I'm off. I'll probably be at Barbara's place for a couple of hours after dinner, so I won't be too late back." Instead of looking at you with her usual cheerful face, Mom looks down at the carpet, her head leans forward and down to one side and her voice seems to have slowed down and aged twenty years as she says, in a world-weary tone, "Oh don't worry, I'll be fine. Just you go ahead and enjoy yourself, and don't give a thought to me at all. I'll be fine."

This is a classic case of the non-verbal cues—body language and tone of voice—being in direct conflict with the spoken words. Mom's non-verbal message is clear: she doesn't want you to go, she would prefer that you didn't enjoy yourself and she has no intention of being fine at all!

It's not only in personal situations that this type of conflict arises. People send non-verbal messages in the workplace all the time, and effective listeners have learned to "hear" them. Note that how you decide to respond is not the issue here—the important thing is that you recognize the underlying message.

There are two types of non-verbal cue: body language and tone of voice.

Body language

Although the body often speaks loudly, its language is not an exact one. There is danger in interpreting individual gestures and mannerisms according to a fixed set of "rules", because they do not always mean the same thing from one person to another. For example, conventional wisdom tells us that folded arms indicate defensiveness or unwillingness to be persuaded; however, many people (including me) fold their arms simply because they find it a comfortable position! Another commonly held belief is that you can't trust someone who doesn't look you in the eye. The problem is, someone who is an accomplished liar probably knows this, and is quite prepared to look you solemnly in the eye and lie quite happily!

So what are we to do? Does this mean body language isn't relevant? No, it doesn't. But it has led to the slightly more reliable measure of "body language clusters". So if your boss stands in front of your desk with arms folded while asking for information, it doesn't necessarily mean anything. But if she folds her arms and at the same time taps her foot, frowns and clenches her teeth—this may be a good time to tread warily in your response to the question!

What the good listener looks for is body language that *seems* to contradict the words the speaker is saying. When they are in direct conflict, usually the body language is a truer indication of meaning.

Tone of voice

Have you ever heard a speaker stand up on the platform and begin a speech with the words, "I'm pleased to be here with you today"—spoken in a flat monotone that indicated no pleasure at all? What was your reaction? You probably noticed that the tone of voice didn't match the words—and you believed the tone. Most people would. What did that do for the speaker's credibility? My guess is: not much.

Tone of voice plays a much more important part in our conversations than we realize. On hearing their voices on a tape recording for the first time, most people refuse to believe they sound "like that". Often, they don't realize that they speak in such a flat tone, but the tape is proof that many of us do.

So how does this information help us listen? Simple: it gives us another tool to evaluate the truth and sincerity of the person's actual words and the feelings behind them. Ideally, for a message to be clear and uncomplicated, the words, body language and tone of voice should all be congruent. In other words, they should all send the same message with no conflict.

Lively listeners always pay attention to the non-verbal cues because they are a vital component of communication.

Rule No. 6: Listen with your whole body

Picture this. Something exciting happened at work today. When you and your partner sit down to dinner, you begin to relate the incident. Your partner doesn't look at you, doesn't say a word, shows no reaction—just looks at the food as it makes its way from plate to mouth. Do you feel listened to? Is your partner using the tools of lively listening? The fact is, that person might well be listening, might be taking in every word you say. But is it lively listening? No.

You see, the lively listener not only takes in information, but indicates in many ways that the speaker's message is indeed getting through. If you want to make it clear that you are listening, use your entire body.

First, *look* at the person speaking. On a recent European vacation, I went to a bank to change some travellers' cheques. The person behind the desk took my passport, went through the entire process and put the local currency down in front of me—and never looked at me once! In fact, I don't know why he bothered to look at the photo in my passport, because he never checked to see if I was the same person! He may well have known exactly what he was doing technically, but as a communicator he failed miserably and he certainly wasn't a lively listener.

Give the speaker the non-verbal feedback we have already discussed: nod your head, smile or frown, vary your expression to suit your response, lean towards the speaker. That way, the speaker is encouraged to continue because you have made it clear you are listening.This honours the speaker.

Using your body also helps you, as you are much less likely to let your attention wander. In other words, by clearly indicating to the speaker that you *are* listening, you will actually improve the *quality* of your listening.

Rule No. 7: Separate fact from opinion and propaganda

It's a few years now since the Internet first began to make its way into our lives, and at first we didn't take much notice. If you are like me, you probably hoped it would go away because it sounded so complicated and technical. But gradually it became more user friendly—even though still complicated and technical—and more and more of us began to make use of it. We surfed, we browsed, we e-mailed. Then, those of us who operate small businesses or work on our own noticed that we were being encouraged (or pushed!) to have our own web pages. Then, insidiously, pundits began to suggest that companies could not survive unless they had "web presence". That is propaganda. And it's not true. At this time, and probably for the foreseeable future, businesses can survive and prosper without advertising their presence on the Worldwide Web. That's opinion too—mine. Of course, it may not be true either.

That's the challenge of Rule No. 7—you must learn to decide what is fact and what is just someone else's opinion or what they would like you to believe. People colour their words in many ways, adding to the challenge of lively listening.

"Everybody does it". This is the bandwagon effect I just described. We are all familiar with what the advertising industry calls "lifestyle advertising". You know the sort of thing: a group of happy, laughing adults enjoying a backyard barbecue beside a sparkling blue swimming pool—all drinking a certain brand of beer. The implication, the suggestion, the unspoken message is that if you drink this beer, you too can enjoy this lifestyle.

Of course, we all recognize this tactic as applied to advertising, but we don't always notice it in normal conversation. Any time someone is trying to persuade you to do something or believe something, listen carefully for the facts and strip away the opinion.

Janice works in a stock brokerage house. By working hard and learning the business, she has steadily moved up to the top of the "non-professional" ranks and makes good money. However, her boss is now encouraging her to go one step further by taking the industry examination that would vault her into the "professional" ranks and open up a whole new world of career possibilities. She is discussing this with her co-worker, Sharon, who has not risen as high or as quickly. Sharon says, "If I were you I wouldn't bother with the exam. *Everybody says* it's too much work. You have to put your life on hold just to pass the exam. And *nobody* ever really gets promotion because of it anyway. Just stay as you are." Janice knows a number of people who have successfully written the exam without giving up their other activities, and several of them have done very well in their careers. So, if she is a lively listener, she can separate what has been said into fact (others have succeeded through taking the exam), and the "bandwagon" propaganda Sharon is presenting.

Another way facts can be distorted is with biased words and expressions. I watched a television documentary about the changing lifestyle of a community on a small island in the South Pacific. At one point, the reporter pushed his microphone in the face of the Chief and said, "How does it feel having decisions about your life made by white governments in London and New York?" Now, judging from the rest of the film, there was little evidence that this was true, but the reporter seemed to feel he would get a more interesting answer by asking his question in these volatile terms. But the old Chief was a lively listener! He simply puffed on his pipe, smiled his ragged-toothed smile and waggled his wrinkled finger at the reporter, as if to say, "You're not going to fool me, Mr. Smart Reporter!"

People sometimes have so much vested interest in their opinions being accepted that they sound like a television evangelist in full swing. "This new process will revolutionize the way our company operates!" they say. That may well be true, but it may not be the kind of revolution you want! Or it may not be true at all. Learn to strip away the opinion and propaganda and listen for the facts before you decide how to respond.

Rule No. 8: Control your emotional response

We all have hot buttons. We all have attitudes and beliefs that make us respond with a sudden flash of anger when people raise certain topics in particular ways. I'll tell you one of mine: racism. Ever since I was a child, I've never understood the rationale behind racism. Why do people hate other people simply because they are a different colour or race, or practise a different religion? To me, it simply doesn't make sense. Over the years, I have read many accounts of poor treatment people have received simply because of their racial background—and it has made me angry and bewildered. It has made me so angry that now I understand it is one of my hot buttons. In fact, as I mature I now realize that this button is so hot for me that sometimes I hear a "racist" remark where none in fact exists. But because I recognize my hot button, a subject with the potential to make me respond emotionally, now I (sometimes!) control this response.

What are *your* hot buttons? It's important to be aware of them so that you can decide how to react when someone pushes them in a conversation.

As a lively listener, you need to take several steps to control your emotional response to what someone says to you.

First, you must recognize your response. When someone says something that makes you angry, what does it feel like? What happens in your body? Usually, one of the first things we notice is a change in our breathing pattern—breathing becomes faster and shallower. Perhaps you find blood rushes to your face and you feel heat there. Some people feel a headache suddenly begin, others automatically ball their hands into fists. (Actually using the fists would be an extreme reaction, but not unknown.) How do you feel when your hot button is pushed? Take some time to really think about this, because it needs to be immediately recognizable to you if you want to be a lively listener.

Now that you know how to recognize an inappropriate emotional response, how do you control it? First, acknowledge it to yourself. This can be a momentary recognition that, yes, this person has said something that is making my blood boil. Just this one step separates you from those who respond blindly and often regret it. Now, take a momentary pause and breathe deeply. This will change your physiological state, while also giving you time to consider what to say. In that split second, you can control yourself and ***choose*** your reaction.

Depending on the subject of the discussion, the person making the remark that has upset you, the purpose of the conversation and other factors, you might take one of three paths.

- Ignore the comment and move on. This might help continue the conversation, or it might simply allow the person's comment to simmer beneath the surface—not a good thing for your wellbeing if done too often. But it is an option.

- Mention it and make an issue of the remark. If the same person constantly presses the same hot button, at some point you will need to do this just to clear the air. It's even possible that the person is doing this unwittingly and only needs to have it pointed out in order to stop.
- Respond in passing and continue the conversation on the right track. For example, in my own case I might say something like, "Although I don't believe the fact that the woman is black has anything to do with the problem, I can see that...". This defuses my own reaction and may well make the person realize the built-in prejudice in the statement, but it does not let the comment distract us from the path of the discussion.

An inappropriate over-reaction can put an end to any conversation, so it is well to learn how to control your emotional response.

Rule No. 9: Make notes

Notes can be on paper, on your computer screen or just in your head, depending on the situation. The important thing is that you make them.

Suppose you are considering buying a new piece of office equipment and have invited a sales person to your office to discuss it. Pull up your pad as the information begins to flow and make notes of important points. This not only gives you the information for future reference, but also may trigger questions for you to ask later in the conversation.

If someone on your staff is explaining a situation and asking for your help, begin by saying, "I'll just make a few notes as we talk" and make it obvious you are doing so. The person now knows you are really listening and paying attention, and the notes serve as focal points to help you formulate your response. Don't overdo the note-taking though. It's one thing to make occasional notes, but if you write down everything the other person will feel like a witness (or a suspect!) undergoing interrogation at police headquarters!

Several years ago I was part of a group of five business women who met once a month to discuss business and provide support for one another. One of the women, Heather, had a fascinating knack of making mental notes. She would be silent for a long period of time while someone was explaining a problem situation, and then, out of the blue, she would refer them to something they had said earlier and use it to redirect or focus their thoughts or come up with new ideas. This facility to make mental notes during the conversation made her a lively listener, and greatly increased the value of her contributions to the group discussions.

Of course, in order to decide which points need to be noted, particularly if you are making mental rather than physical notes, you need to practise the other steps we have already discussed: ask questions, provide feedback, listen with your whole body. All these help elicit information that you can use to make effective notes. Just remember, note-taking is a vital step in becoming a lively listener.

Remember that listening is one part of the Communication Contract©, so it deserves just as much attention as the other communication skills.

Helen's 9 Rules for Lively Listening

1. *Decide to listen.*
2. *Avoid selective listening.*
3. *Give acknowledgement and feedback.*
4. *Ask appropriate questions.*
5. *Listen for non-verbal cues.*
6. *Listen with your whole body.*
7. *Separate fact from opinion and propaganda.*
8. *Control your emotional response.*
9. *Make notes.*

Helen's 9 Rules for Meaningful Meetings

Have you ever sat at a meeting, tuned out of the discussion and thought about all the work you had to do back at your desk? You could be doing next month's budget...you could be doing your sales calls...you could be doing all kinds of things—if only you didn't have to be at this meeting!

People tell me all the time that they can't get on with their work because of the time they spend in meetings. This tells me they think of a meeting not as a part of their work at all, but as an interruption to it. But a meeting can and should be a valuable business tool. There are many issues that can be more effectively dealt with through a meeting than by any other method. To make meetings worthwhile, however, we have to learn to conduct our own better, and also to conduct ourselves better at those held by others.

Much more attention might be given to meeting skills if senior management realized just how much these endless meetings cost organizations every year. Let's just take a look at those costs before we go any further.

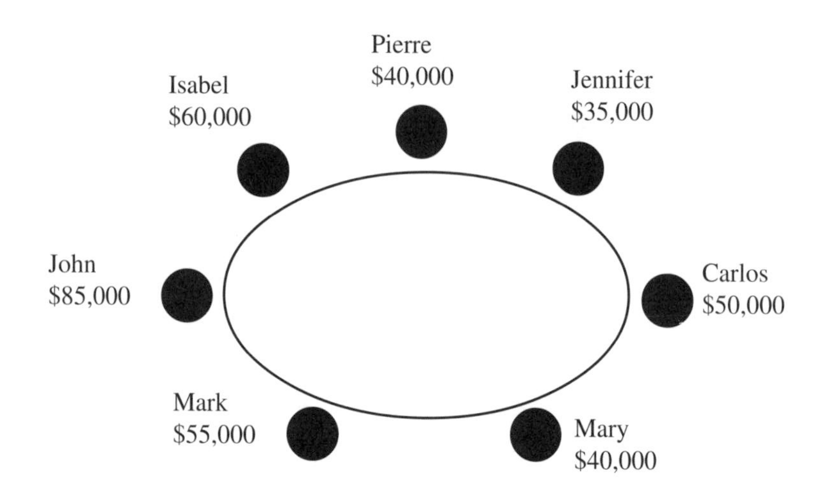

- Above is a graphic representation of a typical middle management meeting in any large corporation today. The figures beside each individual represent annual salaries of the participants, and I have chosen a range to make the example as widely applicable as possible. Notice, no top management salaries are represented here.
- If we total the figures, we find the seven participants represent a total annual salary cost of $365,000. Using the generally accepted norms for working weeks per year, working hours per day, days off and vacations, etc., this translates into an hourly cost of $218. To this we can add a conservative $40 for benefits, bringing the total *salary* cost around the table to $258 per hour.
- Let's assume each person takes half-an-hour to prepare for the meeting, and the meeting itself lasts two-and-a-half hours. That's a relatively short meeting by many standards! Many meetings generate work that must be carried out afterwards, so let's allot one

hour to post-meeting activity. So we can tally the total time spent at this meeting at four hours.

- The total direct cost of these seven people's time for this meeting is, therefore, $1,032.
- But that's only salary. Meetings generate incidental costs: binders, notes, overhead transparencies, coffee and muffins—many employees can't seem to think unless the company provides food! We'll assume $100 for incidentals, a realistic amount. The meeting now costs $1,132.
- It seems reasonable to assume there might be ten such meetings within a major corporation in any given day, which means a total meeting cost per day of $11,320.
- These calculations show that meetings are costing this particular company an average of almost three million dollars per year! And if we factor in those attended by the President and other senior executives, the cost burgeons even higher.

Given these statistics, it is clear that meetings are a costly part of business life. We need to have them, but we must learn to conduct them in such a way that they give organizations a better return on the huge amount of money spent on them every year.

That's the purpose of this section. *Helen's 9 Rules for Meaningful Meetings* focus on ways to make your meetings...well...meaningful!

Rule No. 1: Call only necessary meetings

When I was in the corporate world, there was a verncular term for meetings: "sit down". People would say to each other, "I'll read your report on the proposed project, and then we'll sit down." Trouble was, sometimes that's all they did—they sat down! Nothing much was achieved at these meetings. One major reason: many of the meetings were unnecessary.

Before you call that meeting, ask yourself if it is really necessary, or if your objective could more easily be achieved by another means. What about a series of telephone calls? Could you just send out e-mail messages to the appropriate people? Perhaps even the lowly memo would serve the same purpose. If your purpose is simply to give out information, with little or no two-way interaction, one of these is often the most effective vehicle. Why take busy people away from their desks for a set amount of time (usually too much time) and sit them around a table—just so that you can fire information at them?

On the other hand, action-oriented, decision-making discussions often demand the face-to-face interaction that is only possible at a meeting. So, how do you decide? Here are three indications of the need for a meeting.

Issue under discussion needs input from several people

You must write a report with a recommendation to Management. You call Bob and ask for information, which you receive. But it also brings up a question you hadn't considered before and only Jessica has the answer. When you call, she is out of town for three days but her assistant directs you to Tom. He thinks he knows, but just needs to be sure about one point and he will get back to you as soon as he talks to Jack. And on and on and on. You've been there, haven't you?

This scenario lends itself to a meeting, convened for a time when everyone is available, at which information can be exchanged and discussed to the point where you have all you need for the report and recommendation.

Potential conflicts

There's a very good reason the courts don't allow "hearsay evidence"—it usually can't be trusted, particularly if one party to a conversation is not there to confirm or deny the substance. If you are at all concerned that the issue under discussion is seen in various lights by different interested parties, the best course is to bring them all together and put the issue on the table for discussion. Then there can be no doubt later about what anyone said.

Commitment needed from several people

The Production Department is ready to manufacture the new widget. The Marketing Department has plans in place to put it on the market. Finance has crunched the numbers but still has questions. Are we ready to go? No. The systems people are not sure they can incorporate the new product into the system in the projected time. Steps will need to be taken to resolve the problem, and in the end all departments must commit to their parts in the product launch. A face-to-face meeting is the best platform for discussion of this situation.

One major time waster is the regular meeting. You know—the weekly sales meeting, the monthly departmental get-together, or any other meeting that is always held at the same time in the same place because, well, that's how we always do it. "Because we've always done it" is not a valid reason to hold a meeting. Of course, many of these sessions are worthwhile and much that is good comes out of them. But there are always weeks or months when there is just not a lot to discuss, but somehow we feel we must hold the meeting anyway. Here's one way to break that cycle.

As meeting leader, you first consider what might be on the agenda, including items of varying degrees of importance and urgency. Then, with a reasonable amount of notice, you circulate your "agenda planning notes" to the regular attendees and ask them to add anything they would like to discuss. When it comes back, consider how many items must be discussed by the time of the regular meeting. If there is even one item that can't wait, you must hold the meeting. However, there could be several items on the list, none of which is pressing. Ask yourself if, in total, they represent enough reason for a meeting and if they do, go ahead and hold it. Otherwise, the meeting is not necessary. Suddenly, Monday morning at 9 a.m. opens up on people's schedules for more pressing business. Hold the next meeting only when enough appropriate agenda items have accumulated.

If you hold regular meetings, chances are you will also be subject to that other well known time-waster: the regular report. If people know they are always expected to report, they will do so whether or not they have anything to say. It becomes highly political and people begin to report on items that are of no interest to the others at the meeting; people have even been known to make up things! There are two possible solutions to this problem:

- Let people know that they should report only when they have appropriate information to communicate, and they will not lose any "brownie points" for not reporting.
- Change the agenda so that the regular reports come at the end of the meeting, rather than at the beginning. If you deal with truly important items first, and the regular reports don't come up until it is getting late, you'll be amazed at how short and to-the-point they will become!

One more suggestion for regular meetings: rotate the meeting leadership role. If each participant knows he or she must take a turn at leading, an element of personal pride creeps8in and people do make an effort to run an efficient meeting.

If you have determined that a meeting is indeed necessary, it will be off to the best possible start if you follow the next rule.

Rule No. 2: Invite the right people

Someone has said that meetings are rather like cocktail parties: no-one wants to go, but everyone is offended when not invited!

During the latter years of my corporate experience, I was part of what developed into a meeting fiasco of nightmarish proportions. The setting was a major international oil company, where I was a member of the Corporate Development department. A major project had reached the point where a new company was to be formed, and it was felt appropriate to hold weekly project meetings so that everyone would be up to date on developments. Sounds logical? Oh yes, we thought so too—at first!

Thursday morning at 9 a.m. was chosen as the time for the meetings, and the intention was that they would last an hour or so. Well, the first two or three did anyway. Attendees were: the department head (leader of the meetings), the functional heads of marketing, engineering and finance, the company lawyer (no-one quite knew why he was there but it seemed like a good idea at the time), and me. I was the designated minute taker and the one to make sure everyone did as they said they would after the meetings. It should be noted that these participants constituted the entire department.

The first sign that the meetings were getting off-track was their length. One hour became 90 minutes, which became a regular two hours and more. We developed the deadly practice of regular reports by each manager in turn (whether or not they had anything to report). I must say some of them were quite creative, but that didn't make up for their lack of relevance!

The next problem arose as we began to take on new staff, all of whom were diligently added to the attendee list. An attempt was made to curtail this in one instance, but the people involved became incensed at the perceived slight and the omission was hastily corrected before the next meeting. We then had to move to a larger meeting room and order twice as much coffee. About that time, muffins were added to the menu.

Somewhere along the line, we moved out of Head Office into our own space at another location. Then the Thursday meeting really came into its own. Picture a large, conference room with u-shaped table arrangement, with approximately twenty people in attendance. It had taken on the proportions of one of those series of endless peace talks among warring peoples. The only staff member not attending the meeting was one secretary, who was left to handle all incoming calls while at the same time keeping the coffee flowing for a meeting which now needed lunch to be ordered in and had become almost a whole-day affair!

As was common with oil companies in the glorious, booming eighties, these people were all well paid. I have never quite had the courage to try to calculate exactly what these meetings cost in dollars, but they certainly took a heavy toll in nerves and patience.

What went wrong? Well, a number of things did, but they could all probably have been overcome if we hadn't broken rule No. 2: invite the right people. We didn't worry about whether they were the right people—whether they had anything to contribute or not—we simply invited everyone as a matter of course. Please don't make this mistake.

So, who are the right people for your meeting? Here are a few criteria.

- They have knowledge to contribute. In light of the agenda, who has the necessary knowledge and information to move the meeting towards its objective? Who can contribute to a meaningful discussion that leads to a satisfactory conclusion? They should be invited.
- They should have authority or influence in the area under discussion. Don't invite people just because they have rank. If the meeting is to discuss topics outside their sphere of influence, they won't be meaningful contributors and they probably will not thank you for taking up their time.
- They should be willing to spend the necessary time to be at the meeting. Nothing is more destructive to the collective will of a meeting than someone who keeps checking the time and showing other obvious signs of impatience.
- They should not only be willing to express their viewpoints, but also be open to listening to those of other participants.

If you have decided your meeting is necessary and have invited those who are most likely to contribute to its success, give your meeting another advantage by following the next rule.

Rule No. 3: Distribute the Agenda Before the Meeting

I'm constantly amazed at the number of business meetings called every day without an agenda. It's a recipe for disaster. No wonder so many meetings ramble on aimlessly—they have no idea where they are supposed to be going in the first place because there is no agenda.

Notice, this rule doesn't just say you need an agenda. It says ***distribute it before the meeting***. That means, of course, it must be written down! A list of items in the leader's mind does not an agenda make.

Receiving a copy of an agenda just as you walk into a meeting is almost as useless as not having one—not quite, but almost. Although you now know what is to be discussed, you have had no time to prepare for your own involvement. If, on the other hand, you receive an agenda in advance, you can collect relevant material from your files, contact other people where necessary for further information, perhaps even prepare written handouts to help the discussion.

When you distribute the agenda, ask recipients for their suggested additions. Make it clear that whoever adds an item will be expected to lead the dicussion of that topic. This simple tactic will stop people from adding unnecessary items.

When all suggestions are received, make a final version of the agenda, with time allotted to each item, and distribute it to participants again.

All agendas are not created equal

The wording used in the agenda can have an impact on the success of the meeting. I strongly believe in telling people the *purpose* of the meeting, in advance. You can do this in your cover memo or, as I prefer, right at the top of the agenda itself. Note, the wording of the purpose is important.

Poor: The purpose of the meeting is to discuss possible ways of reducing next year's expenses.

Good: At this meeting we will (a) identify means of reducing next year's expense budget by 10%, and (b) set an implementation schedule.

Any talk of *discussing, considering or* (shudder) *stick handling* is an invitation to a long, rambling meeting that achieves nothing. Remember, a stimulating conversation is one thing, but a successful meeting is another: the latter must achieve its stated objective.

Instead, base your agenda on strong, powerful verbs that describe a measurable objective.

- ***Agree*** on date, time and venue for annual conference
- ***Compile*** list of requirements for new office space
- ***Complete*** job description for Vice President Marketing
- ***Draft*** purchase offer for 50% of shares in ACME Widgets

All of these agenda items are measurable: you will either achieve them or not. That makes it easier to keep the discussion on track—more on that later.

ꞮT AND FINISH ON TIME

of attention is given (often with little to show for it) gs on time. Just as important to their success, *ing* on time. What do I mean by finishing on time? specified on the agenda. Oh, you didn't know you ng time? Let me tell you a little story.

Several years ago I served on a volunteer committee at my church. Now, I don't know if you have experience of working with volunteers, but very often (certainly in a church environment) the work done is just part of the reason people volunteer their time and effort. A large part of it is also social in nature. People like to get together and feel they are doing something worthwhile at the same time. There's nothing wrong with that, of course, but it often makes it difficult to run things in a businesslike manner. This particular committee had a terrible reputation. Monthly meetings began at 7.30 p.m. and often dragged on until after 11 p.m., and to make matters worse, usually little was accomplished. Members changed regularly because people were frustrated. I was almost at the point of leaving, when I heard someone new was taking over the chair. I didn't know the woman, but I thought I'd give it another chance.

When I arrived at the next meeting and met the new leader, my heart sank. She was a soft-spoken, elderly woman who looked as if she could be knocked down by a feather. My reaction was: game over—she'll never stand up to this group and things will get even worse. Was I wrong! This tiny person ran those meetings with an iron fist. Within the first three months, the meetings were ticking along, agenda items were dealt with and we left by 9.45 p.m. every time. What a difference! How did she do it? Simple: she had a system which she followed strictly, and it began with a properly designed agenda—which, of course, was distributed ahead of the meetings.

The key was that each item on the agenda was allotted a specific time for discussion, and that time was marked on the agenda. I remember well that first meeting. The lady began by saying we would begin the practice of finishing the meetings at 9.45 p.m. sharp. (Nobody believed her of course.) At about ten past eight, we were in full flight as usual, rambling around a topic and getting nowhere. Our fearless new leader interrupted, saying, "Excuse me, but our agenda calls for discussion of this topic to end at 8.15 p.m. That gives us another five minutes. Would you like to end the discussion there, and continue it if necessary next month, or would you like to carry on? In that case, of course, we will need to take something else off the agenda to compensate for the extra time." We finished in five minutes! The leader repeated this procedure several times throughout the evening. She gave us her final five minute warning at 9.40 p.m., and at precisely 9.45 p.m. she said, "Thank you. Our meeting is now at an end. Let us pray." The minister was quite taken by surprise, but he managed to rise to the occasion and, after duly giving thanks for the success of our endeavours, we did indeed adjourn at 9.45 p.m.

And so it continued. For the first couple of meetings we didn't quite finish our agenda items. But after that, people just somehow fell into line and the committee took on a new lease on life.

You can perform the same miracle in your business meetings. Set a realistic discussion time for each item. The exercise of setting these times will force you to realize when you have tried to include too many items—a common fault with business meetings. When people know they will be free by the time stated on the agenda, they will not be reluctant to devote the time to your meeting.

Rule No. 5: State the Objective at the Start of the Meeting

As meeting leader, you should begin by thanking everyone for coming, and then go on to state clearly the reason for the meeting. Of course, you have already done this on your agenda, but by restating it at the start of the proceedings you will remind the attendees why they are there, and demonstrate that you intend to run an efficient meeting whose results will be measurable.

In stating your objective, say what you want to achieve.

Poor: We are here to consider
We need to discuss
The purpose of this meeting is to review

Good: We are here to determine
Today we must reach a consensus on
At today's meeting we will set the schedule for

By stating the objective in the form of a measurable goal, you allow each attendee to focus on his or her participation in the discussion.

Take the opportunity to verbally summarize the agenda, emphasizing that the meeting will be adjourned at the pre-determined finishing time. This sets the tone for an efficient, orderly, businesslike discussion. It also makes it clear that you are in control and intend to "run a tight ship".

Having an objective at all is a step beyond many business meetings, and leads us directly to the next rule.

Rule No. 6: Keep the meeting moving towards its objective

As I have already said, there is a big difference between an interesting discussion and an effective meeting. A good leader knows how to achieve the latter by smoothly guiding the discussion.

Think for a moment of how an orchestra depends on the conductor. Every musician knows his or her individual part of the music, but without the conductor they would all go at varying speeds, perhaps inserting their own improvisation, and rarely finish at the same time. Along the way, the clashes would completely spoil the music.

In a meeting, the leader is the conductor, without whose firm hand the meeting is likely to go off in all directions and never meet its objective. Here are a few tips on how to keep your meeting on track.

- If specialized knowledge or specific information is needed, make sure the attendees include at least one person who can supply it. Few meeting woes are more frustrating than having a detailed discussion come to nothing because nobody present could supply needed data on which to base a decision. The specialist might be someone from another department or even from outside the organization. This person may need to attend only for part of the discussion, but it is crucial to have the input available.
- Some people are born critics. You've probably run into certain people at meetings who always disagree with any proposal on the table. They always have a problem with every suggestion—and never, of course, have suggestions of their own to offer. Typically, their body language demonstrates their attitude: folded arms, slight condescending sneer, rueful shaking of the head. These people are always, as my mother used to say, "agin the government". The best way to handle them is to make them prove their point:

  — *I can see you don't agree, John. What is your specific problem with this idea?*

  — *Janice, since you evidently don't go along with the plan, can you explain to us what the difficulty is?*

  — *You've mentioned several times that this won't work, George, but can you explain exactly why not?*

  If you do this every time, they will soon grow tired of having to justify themselves and begin to think before automatically disagreeing with everyone. Don't forget too, when one person is a nuisance in this way, everyone else will be on your side and happy to have the troublemaker silenced.

- Side issues can arise in the midst of discussions, completely throwing the agenda off track. Suppose, for example, your professional firm has agreed to hold a client seminar as part of the marketing effort. The following discussion follows the initial decision:

Jan: "Where shall we hold it?"
Bob: "In the main boardroom I guess."
Jan: "Oh no, surely not. There's not nearly enough room."
Bob: "Yes there is. That room holds easily twenty people, and..."
Bill: "Twenty! We need a lot more than that to make this work. I see at least seventy."
Bob: "Seventy? Who are all these people?
Bill: "Clients, prospects....."
Jan: "But we'll never have space to serve food to all those..."
Liz: "Oh no, are we having food? Let's not have finger food this time—remember the disaster at that client meeting last summer?"
Bill: "That new sushi place does great takeout food..."
Liz: "Yes but some people are allergic to seafood. My Auntie Mary once ate..."

Can you see where this is going? Have you been in on one of those rambling discussions? All these things need to be discussed, but this meeting is probably not the place, especially if other pressing matters are on the agenda. Solution? Appoint a committee to handle the details and logistics. Set a date and time for them to report back to the group with decisions on time, place, numbers, catering and other logistical details. *Then move on to the next agenda item.*

- Discussions can grow too long for several reasons: some people like the sound of their own voices; many never use one word when ten would do; some like to restate everything for their own or others' clarification; topics turn out to be more intricate than expected. If you are to stay on track, however, you must find a way to avoid endless discussion. The most obvious way is to limit the length of speaking time for each person: "I'm sorry Mary, but that is your quota of speaking time for this topic and we need to move on so that everyone can contribute." Be scrupulously fair in applying this remedy and nobody should take offence. (Some will, of course, but nobody should!)
- What if discussion shows no sign of waning because of a variety of opinions? A simple way to end discussion is to take a vote. You may vote on whether to continue the discussion at another time, perhaps with written submissions beforehand; or you may vote on the decision itself. In any case, a vote is a time-honoured method of closing a discussion.

One question I am often asked is how to deal with people who hog the floor. We've all experienced a meeting where one or more of those attending have so much to say that others don't get a chance to voice their opinions. As the leader, you should insist that attendees raise their hands to indicate they want to speak, instead of simply plunging in. Try to take speakers in the order they raised their hands, but if you have some floor hoggers in the group, just mention that you would like to hear from some of the others. You might say something like, "Mark, hold that thought if you would. I just want us to hear from the others first before we come back to you." This lets Mark know he will have his opportunity to speak again, making it more likely he will actually pay attention to what others have to say first.

One type of participant who can be a potential meeting disrupter is the one whose statements and questions have nothing to do with the subject under discussion. This can be perplexing, because it can lead the discussion so far off track that it is difficult to bring it back. The key is to make the speaker identify the connection before responding to the question or comment. You can do this politely: "I'm sorry Jennifer, but I'm not quite sure how that ties in with our discussion about changing the production schedule. Could you explain the connection before we discuss your point?"

If you are to make meetings work for you on any level, you must adhere to the next rule.

Rule No. 7: Don't just sit there—say something!

Besides the greater good of achieving an objective, business meetings present an opportunity to influence conditions; to raise your profile; to further your career—but *only* if you contribute. Just sitting there like a bump on a log while others do the talking will get you nowhere. Here are a few tips on how to make your mark at meetings.

Arrive early so that you can get the best seat. What is the best seat? Well, that depends on your plans for the meeting. If you want the leader to notice you and single you out for your views, sit opposite the leader. When he or she looks up from agenda, notes, etc. you will be the first person in the line of sight, and you'll often be asked to comment. If, on the other hand, you would like a little more time to think before speaking, or prefer to be more of an observer at this particular meeting, sit to one side of the leader.

Comfort reduces energy level. If there's a choice between a soft, comfy armchair and a straight-backed, firm chair—choose the latter. Draw your chair up to the conference table and sit up straight, not slumped back or over one arm. Leaning forward slightly over the table signals that you are alert and ready to participate.

Don't hesitate to jump in when you have something to say. Perhaps you've been in a position where you thought you might have a worthwhile suggestion to add to the discussion, but didn't quite have the confidence to offer it so you kept quiet. Two minutes later, someone else put forward exactly your suggestion—and everyone thought it was brilliant! Now what?

You can't say, "Oh, I was just going to say that!" As professional business speaker Patricia Fripp says, "If you have a good idea but lack the confidence to talk about it, you won't get credit for having had it." So go ahead and speak—that's what a meeting is for.

If you are shy and lack confidence, make a point of speaking early in the meeting. Say *something*, even if it's less than earth- shattering. For example, ask for another copy of the agenda; ask if anyone else feels warm and suggest lowering the heat. Anything,well, within reason! The point is, once you've spoken the first time, it becomes less inhibiting to join in the discussion in a more meaningful way throughout the meeting.

What happens after a meeting can be vital, which brings us to the next rule.

Rule No. 8: Arrange for appropriate notes

Notice, I don't say you should *take* appropriate notes, but rather arrange for someone else to do so. It's very difficult to lead a meeting, or even take a significant part in the discussion, and take useful notes or minutes at the same time. A long time ago I developed an interest in photography. Back then I was also keen on hockey, so I took my camera along to an NHL game, planning to catch some exciting action shots. I soon found I either had to take the pictures and forget about the game, or cheer my team on and sacrifice the photographs. You can't take pictures and watch the game at the same time. The same applies to minute taking.

If the meeting is important enough to take the participants away from their desks, surely a secretary can also be spared to take the notes. Usually in business, formal parliamentary-type minutes are not necessary, but it is essential that someone keep track of decisions and action items. The person who takes the notes should also be responsible for following up with those designated to take action, to make sure they do so. When a specific action is to be taken, the notes should clearly say what it is, who is to do it and, whenever possible, the target date for completion. Everyone attending the meeting should receive a copy of the notes as soon after the meeting as possible.

Whether by means of a formal minute book or a simple file folder, copies of the notes should be kept together in a place where they can be readily retrieved if necessary. That way they form a permanent record as well as a tool for making sure things are done.

If the meeting is a formal one where decisions will be made by resolution, it is vital that the wording be accurately recorded and verified. After discussion, the secretary should read out the resolution as it will appear in the minutes. Only when the proposer and seconder are satisfied that the resolution accurately represents the desired decision should the vote take place.

Rule No. 9: When the objective has been accomplished—stop!

Accomplishing your meeting objective is an achievement. After all, this is the reason you all left your desks and came together for this period of time. You set aside two hours away from the rest of your work to settle this question, and you have done so—with half an hour to spare. In this situation, rather than celebrate a job well done, too many managers instead begin to discuss something else. By doing this, you take away the well deserved feeling of accomplishment the attendees should enjoy.

Rather, congratulate the group on a job well done and sincerely express your appreciation. Everyone will leave feeling good about themselves, about you as a leader—and about future meetings you will hold.

Internal meetings are an integral part of business life. They have a function that cannot easily be replaced by any other means and I don't suggest for a moment that they are not necessary. What I do stress, however, is that they are expensive and if they are to be cost-effective we must learn to run them efficiently.

Helen's 9 Rules for Meaningful Meetings

1. ***Call only necessary meetings.***
2. ***Invite the right people.***
3. ***Distribute the agenda before the meeting.***
4. ***Start and finish on time.***
5. ***State the objective at the start of the meeting.***
6. ***Keep the meeting moving towards its objective.***
7. ***Don't just sit there—say something!***
8. ***Arrange for appropriate notes.***
9. ***When the objective has been accomplished—stop!***

Helen's 9 Rules for Publishable Prose

So it wasn't enough for you to practise your profession: now your firm wants you to be a journalist too? Well, not quite. But it is true that article writing is becoming more and more a part of the daily lives of many professionals.

I'm sure you have noticed that those who not only practise their profession but actually bring in the business to the firm—the Rainmakers—are the ones with the illustrious careers. There are, of course, many things you must do to become a Rainmaker, but the single most important thing is that you must raise your profile and become well known in your field.

This section is designed to help you take what could be your first step toward Rainmaker status: writing and publishing articles. It really isn't as daunting as you think. All you need are some guidelines to follow and that's what *Helen's 9 Rules for Publishable Prose* are. These rules deal not only with writing the material, but also how to take that essential leap from *your* printed page to the *magazine's* printed page.

Rule No. 1: Target the publication *before* you write the article.

Would you ever consider writing a report and then looking for a client to fit it? I seriously doubt it. But that's what professionals of all kinds do all the time, when they write an article about some area of their expertise and then try to find a magazine that will publish it. That's the wrong approach.

Don't try to sell a canned, pre-packaged article, because not all the facts about your topic will fit all publications. You must first decide what magazine you want to write for, and write the piece for that magazine's readers.

So, how do you find the right magazine? First ask yourself who you want to reach with your message. Are they your clients or prospects? The general public? Students of your profession?

Now ask yourself another question: what do these people read? As a business person, your first thought is probably the business press. That is valid, but it is just the beginning. Perhaps you want to reach potential clients for your business among corporate executives. Of course they do read business magazines and newspapers. But remember, besides being corporate icons, these are real people, with real interests outside the office. A large percentage, for example, play golf and read golf magazines. If they travel, they read in-flight publications. They might have hobbies of all kinds such as boating, horseback riding, skiing, radio-controlled model building, and you can reach them through the myriad magazines devoted to these special interests. So don't limit yourself when considering what publications to target.

You can probably come up with quite a few ideas by thinking along these lines. You can get a few more by checking out the magazine racks in your local bookstore. But you need a more systematic approach if you are going to make article writing an ongoing part of your marketing efforts. If you want to write for Canadian magazines, you need to become familiar with an invaluable publication called *Canadian Advertising Rates and Data*, commonly known as C.A.R.D. For the American market, check the U.S. equivalent of C.A.R.D., called *Standard Rates & Data Service*. You can find both in any good sized public library. For more information on C.A.R.D., check its website at www.cardmedia.com. The S.R.D.S. website is www.srds.com.

Both books are large directories, listing virtually every publication in their respective countries, sorted by publication type and subject matter. In these books you'll find newspapers, consumer magazines, trade magazines, professional publications, radio and television stations. The listings give details of the editorial staff, contact addresses and telephone numbers. But even more important for your purposes are the demographics of readership and the type of content the publications offer. This is the information you need in order to decide which publications would be best for you to target for your professional articles, and it is part of every listing in C.A.R.D.

After a close examination of the directory of your choice, you can make a list of publications that interest you. Now you need to become familiar with each one on your list.

The first thing to do is to call each publication and ask for its writers' guidelines (sometimes known as writers' tipsheets), which they will be pleased to send to you. These vary in style from a single sheet to elaborate packages of full colour printed materials, but it is essential that you get them. The writers' guidelines tell you what type of material the magazine needs, what kind of treatment or approach they like, the length of articles and lots of other pertinent information. You *must* pay attention to these needs if you want to be published.

Besides the writers' guidelines, you should also ask for a sample issue of the publication. Some include this automatically as part of the package, but you should ask for it specifically. Most will not expect payment for this sample, but you should offer to pay and ask them to send you an invoice. (I have never actually been asked to pay for a sample issue, but I always offer and I am prepared to pay.)

It is important to read at least this one issue of the magazine, because you'll want to get a feel for the editorial style as well as subject matter. If possible, try to scan a number of back issues, which are often available at the library or on the publication's website. This not only lets you become even more familiar with the publication style but also the subjects it has recently covered, so you won't offer something they covered just a couple of issues ago.

If you follow these steps, you will now be ready for the next rule.

Rule No. 2: Plan your article for those particular readers

What aspect of your topic is suitable for this magazine? How could you slant your story so that this magazine's readers would be interested in it? To make it easier, personalize the reader in your mind's eye. Is the reader your mother? your brother-in-law the dentist? a prominent member of your professional group or industry sector? the guy who fixes your car? What would this person need to know about your topic?

Imagine, for example, you are a lawyer and you want to write about some recent changes in automobile insurance regulations. If you wrote for a consumer magazine, you would need to talk about how the changes affect drivers. Insurance trade magazine readers would be more likely to want to know how changes affect insurers. Autobody trade magazine readers would want to know how the new regulations would affect the way insurance companies pay for repairs. You must be clear about what you have to say to *this particular magazine's readers*.

Don't bring in side issues. People are often tempted to put in information just because they have it. Don't. It will be edited out anyway, and it won't endear you to the editor.

So now you know what you want to write and for which publication. But do they want your story? Find out by following the next rule.

Rule No. 3: Query First

The query is a standard component in the publication process. You can do it by letter, phone or e-mail. If you decide to call, plan first what you will say because editors are busy people and you will only have a few minutes to interest them in your proposition. Personally, I am more comfortable writing first, but I know other writers who prefer the phone call. In fact, what matters is the editor's preference, and writers' guidelines often give this information. If they don't, you might call the magazine and ask.

This is where C.A.R.D. and S.R.D.S. come in handy again. Find the name of the appropriate editor in the book, and then call to confirm. People in publishing tend to move around a lot, so it's important to make sure you are writing to the person currently in the position. Large publications often have more than one editor. They might have a business editor, a features editor, a women's editor, etc. Choose the appropriate one and get the person's name. Query letters that begin "Dear Editor" are off to a poor start.

When you are trying to interest an editor in your article, remember you must offer a story, not just a topic. This is what journalists mean by a "hook" or an "angle". For example, "New automobile insurance regulations" is not a story. "You can't sue the other guy for millions any more" might be. When studying your sample issue, look at the type of angle the magazine stories have. You will have a better chance of success if you follow the same style.

No matter the form of your query, it must tell the editor three things:

- the subject of the story
- why readers will be interested in it
- why you should be the one to write it.

On the next page is a sample query letter our fictitious lawyer might write to the editor of a consumer magazine. Read it and see how it answers these questions. You can adapt this sample to fit your own purposes, or write your own, just as long as it gives the editor the necessary information.

Dear [editor's name]:

Recent changes in automobile insurance regulations have many people upset and confused. I would like to write an article for [name of publication] that explains simply and clearly how they can tell whether or not they are affected and what they must do to comply.

Through the stories of four very different road accidents, I will illustrate the difference between the old and the new regulations. I will relate how the drivers' insurance coverage protected them then, and how different the results would be under the new regulations.

The piece will be approximately 2,500 words. I can also provide some facts and figures on accident costs under both sets of rules, which might work well as a sidebar.

My practice at [name of your firm] involves me in many insurance-related matters, and my clients include both insurers and insureds. This story would be told from a consumer viewpoint.

I will telephone you next week to see if this interests you. If you would like to speak to me in the meantime, please call my direct line at 987-6543.

Sincerely,

Let's assume, then, that you are successful and the editor bites—you've got the assignment. Now what? Now you start writing!

This is where many professionals get bogged down, but you don't have to be overwhelmed if you know about the next little trick.

Rule No. 4: Tap the power of the formula

We are all familiar with writing formulas, even though we may never think about them. Take, for example, detective fiction. I am a big fan of the traditional "English" detective story, and its formula is very tight. The book starts off by setting the scene, often in a quiet English village where violent crime would be the last thing expected. The cast of characters is introduced, their relationship to one another explored. Then comes the discovery of the body. There's no emphasis here on blood and horror, because the focus of the story is the solution rather than the crime itself. At this point we are introduced to the protagonist: perhaps a private detective, an amateur sleuth or a police type—often a recurring character in the author's books. Then comes the serious business of investigation and we can start to think for ourselves who might be the guilty party. Then, about midway through the story, there is another murder. This is mandatory. Often the detective appears to be in some personal danger. And so on, and so on.... Traditionally, the final act takes place in a spot where all the characters can gather—sometimes a country manor house or high class hotel—where the great detective gets to show off a bit while revealing the details of the crime in very dramatic fashion. Anyway, you get the idea.

This is a formula, and if the author were to deviate from it, the book would not be published because the editors know what their readers want—and what they want is contained within the established formula.

Far from creating problems for authors, this actually makes the writing task easier—and so it can be for you when you begin to write your professional article for publication.

Let me talk about just a few possible formulas for your article. As you read, start thinking about how your topc might fit one or more and which one would be best for any given market.

The List

—*Four ways to make sure you get the best deal on your mortgage*
—*Six questions to ask before hiring an accountant*
—*Helen's 9 Rules for Publishable Prose.*

If you have a number of points about your topic, a list is often the easiest way to sort them. The individual section format allows you to put unrelated facts together in a way that makes them into a system. It is also a format that is easy for people to absorb and remember. Readers like that, making it popular also with editors.

Don't choose the number first. What you do is write down and elaborate on your points one by one, and whatever number you come up with is the number in your title. Of course, you can have a list formula without actually numbering the points. In this case, you must pay more attention to creating smooth transitions between them. Your title will not reflect any number, but by following the list in your mind you will still find it relatively simple to write.

Burst the Bubble

This formula is useful when you want to introduce a new and better product, service or way of doing things. First you blow the bubble, by describing the existing way in some detail. Then you burst it by pointing out the faults, problems and difficulties. This, of course, sets the scene for you to introduce the new approach.

Short Case Studies

The story we proposed in our sample query letter earlier is an example of this formula. We proposed to tell the stories of four different accidents, using each to illustrate the old and new auto insurance regulations. Each story would be a mini case study. The formula can be adapted in length and detail, depending on the number of words allotted to the whole story.

When you do this, take the opportunity to use people in your stories whenever possible. A professional paper can talk in abstract concepts, but a story is about people. This is true even when you are writing for a professional magazine read by your peers. People always bring a story to life.

The Interview

If you know your readers well, you will have some idea of the questions they would like to ask on the topic. Simply state the questions, then answer them. For example, if you are a real estate appraiser writing a story on what to look for in a new house, you might ask questions such as:

— *How can you tell if the roof is sound?*
— *When is building an extension more practical than buying a bigger house?*
— *Is a swimming pool an asset or a liability when it's time to sell?*

Surveys and Studies

Surveys can be a useful marketing tool, and the findings make interesting articles. You might, for example, write something based on:

— *More and more companies are using contract employees because....*
— *Debit cards are becoming the payment form of choice for more people in more markets than ever before.*

You can use the results of studies done by others, quoting them with permission of course. Even better, though, is doing the study yourself. Remember, survey authors carry clout. People will begin to quote the results, and you will automatically be regarded as an expert on the topic. You may even be interviewed by others writing articles, such as professional journalists, and quoted in the press. This can be a major step in your journey to Rainmaker status!

Well, have you had any ideas yet about which formula to use for your story? There are others, which you will spot if you begin to study magazine articles and look for them, but these are a good start.

Now that you know the subject and shape of your story, you can finally begin to write it. In doing so, pay particular attention to the next rule.

Rule No. 5: Use appropriate language

This means appropriate language *for these readers*. Once again, personalize the readers in your mind and think of how they would express themselves or what type of writing would make them comfortable enough to read your story.

The Wall Street Journal is quite different from your local community newspaper; women who choose *Redbook* or *Chatelaine* for their recreational reading expect quite a different style from those who read *The Economist*; even though both publications often showcase beautiful homes, *Architectural Digest* speaks in quite a different tone from *Better Homes and Gardens*.

In setting your tone, take your cue from the magazine itself. Carefully examine the stories in your sample issue. Is the language formal or casual?

If the magazine uses "you" centred, everyday language, you won't get far with high-flown technical terms. On the other hand, certain learned academic or professional journals won't thank you for breezy, humorous anecdotes.

If it is a special interest magazine, what level of jargon is used? Match your own story with this, and when in doubt err on the side of simplicity.

If you are writing for people in your own industry or profession, a certain amount of jargon is acceptable. However, it's worth remembering that people read magazines, even professional ones, to at least some extent for recreation. So, even though they will know what the technical terms mean, staying with simple language will make your story easier to read. Reading your article should never seem like work.

When writing for consumer publications, stay away from technical language altogether. Towards the end of every year in Canada, financial services companies begin touting their own particular Registered Retirement Savings Plans. These sales pitches are aimed at large segments of the population who often make no other investments, who understand little about finance and who spend the last two months of the year in a dazed state of panic because they can't get the straight goods on which RRSP to buy. If this is your field, remember that unsophisticated investors don't care how many assets you have under management. Apart from having to stop to figure out what it means, they don't know what difference it makes in how you can manage their money. Stay with the basics, and use simple language anyone can understand—at least if you want a professional editor who understands his or her readers to publish your story.

Consideration of tone and language takes us naturally to the next rule.

Rule No. 6: Remember, it's a story

This is not a business report. It's not a memo, a procedure manual or an academic paper. It's a story. If you write it as if you were telling it to a friend on the golf course, you'll come close to the right approach. There are a number of things to remember about writing a story that an editor will want to publish.

Don't bore your readers!

This should be self-evident, of course, but if you read some professional articles in in-house newsletters (which are not subject to outside editing and veto!) you will see that it is not. Magazine readers are not a captive audience—if your story doesn't interest them they will simply turn the page to the next one. There are two simple ways to avoid boring your readers: reader-friendly language and relevant content.

Forget the courtroom

This advice is not only for lawyers. Many professionals are so concerned about people acting on their "advice" that they use language designed to stand up in court. This is not a court document—it's a story. Put in a disclaimer, telling people if they want specific advice they should seek out a consultant (preferably you, of course!) and then relax and tell your story.

Use personal stories

You can bring dry information to life by using people in your story. If you are in real estate, talk about a young couple buying their first home to illustrate some of the problems home buyers encounter. Human Resources professionals sometimes write as if the "human" part of their name didn't exist—illustrate how benefits work by giving examples using people. Even statistics can be made human by giving the figures first and following with a "for example" story. This is equivalent to looking at a long view of a field and then looking through binoculars to find a child playing with the daisies—it adds human interest.

Set up your topic quickly

In journalistic parlance, the first paragraph of your story is called the lead. As its name suggests, it is supposed to lead the readers into the story in such a way that they want to continue reading it. In writing articles, you don't have the luxury of using long background introductions.

I once edited a client's article called *Women in Welding*. This was an interesting look at how some women had successfully penetrated a trade traditionally filled by men, and the first paragraph went on at some length about that tradition. In reading the draft, I found stories of some individual women, one of whom had been a trained and practising nurse before switching to welding. I found that switch to be quite a dramatic one, and the lead became: *Mary Smith used to be a nurse. Now she's a welder.*

Don't waste your reader's time—cut to the chase.

Eliminate anything that slows down the pace

Another client, an engineering firm, asked me to edit their newsletter. One story told of a major engineering project that had made a huge difference in the life of a small town. In the middle of the story the writer had inserted a paragraph containing technical information. This data was of interest to some of the readers, but it stopped the narrative short, so it had no place in the body of the story.

I simply took it out of the body of the story and put it in as a sidebar, so those who wanted the details could read them after they had finished the story. A sidebar, as the name suggests, is simply a section of up to a few paragraphs which is on another aspect of the main topic, or another topic that is somehow connected. It is usually set off in a box, which can be off to one side of the article or embedded in the text.

Let your attitude show

Editors love opinion pieces. Don't be afraid to show how you feel about an issue. It makes for a more interesting story than a bland statement of the facts.

Take out anything not relevant to *this* audience

If you don't, the editor will.

Style

After you have written your first draft, examine the piece carefully for style. Again, there are a number of things to look for:

- **Grammatical and typographical errors**
  There is no excuse for these. Don't expect the editor to clean them up for you—that's not an editor's job.
- **The rhythm of your sentences**
  Use a blend of long and short sentences. Too many short ones in a row will create a choppy feeling in the text, which is uncomfortable to read. Too many long ones can obscure the meaning and also make for tedious reading.
- **The length of your paragraphs**
  In magazine stories, paragraphs should be predominantly short. Think of the layout of a magazine page: often there are three or more narrow columns, so long paragraphs look endless and are offputting to readers.
- **Repetition of words and phrases**
  Find different ways of expressing ideas. Repetition is tedious.
- **Wasted words**

> Editors usually ask for articles of a certain number of words, but they can recognize when you are padding to fill the word count. Take out the fluff.

Who should read your draft? Usually, the first idea is to give it to a colleague in your firm. That is all right, but it can be a two-edged sword.

First, colleagues are likely to use the same jargon as you do, so won't be likely to see it as the barrier to communication it really might be. Second, colleagues might have hidden agendas that prevent them from giving you honest feedback. Third, some people find it impossible to refrain from "wordsmithing" someone else's work, which is at best intimidating and at worst infuriating.

The best reader of your draft is the intended reader of the story. If your target readers are insurance company executives, chances are you know people in the industry. Ask them to look at your manuscript and give you their impressions. Specifically ask for comments on things they don't understand or relate to.

This may surprise you, but an excellent person to review your draft is an intelligent teenager of sixteen or older. If that person understands the gist of your story, and finds it at least somewhat interesting, you are off to a good start.

It's important to realize, however, that your first draft is not the story you submit to the publication. You must edit and polish it from all angles until you are sure you have the best possible product. Then send it off and wait for the comments.

This leads us into the next rule.

Rule No. 7: Don't fight the editor

My husband has an expression to describe someone who holds all the advantages in a given situation. He says that person holds both the cheese and the knife in hand. In your case, the person with the cheese and the knife is the editor.

The editor is the boss, and if you don't play according to his or her rules, you simply won't be published. Many professionals are shocked when first confronted with someone who sends their work back for changes, because they have never met this situation in their own firms. Well, get used to it because it is part of the publishing world.

It's only right that the editor has this power because nobody knows the readers as the editor does. Readers are often fickle, and must always be provided with the material they want. Editors see to it that they are.

There is another concept that may be new or strange to professionals, but worth remembering: editing is not an insult. The editor's job is to make sure the finished article is as good as it can be for this audience, and good professional editing always improves good writing. So don't feel insulted when the editor edits!

Someone from the publication may call you to ask for your sources for certain information, or to confirm facts. This is also normal. Many publications employ people called "fact checkers" to make sure they don't publish inaccurate information. Again, co-operate with these people and make it easy for them to do their jobs.

Rule No. 8: Ask for full attribution

Remember why you are publishing in the first place: to raise your profile, showcase your expertise and, ultimately, support your marketing program. Although not the only measure of your publishing success, the most desirable result is to have a potential client call you after reading your article. This can happen only if the article is followed by contact information. This is called *attribution.* It's usually a short paragraph, printed in italics, immediately after the article. It tells who the author is, sometimes his or her affiliation and how to contact the author. Ideally, telephone, fax or e-mail numbers are provided. Some magazines also include a photograph of the author.

You want this information to be as full as possible. The best way to get the wording you want is simple: write it yourself. When I submit an article for publication, I simply type the attribution paragraph in italics at the end. Of course, you won't always get what you want. Publications have varying policies on what and how much detail they print, but you might as well go for what you want and then take the best you can get.

The ideal attribution mentions your name, your firm name, contact information and your expertise in this particular field. Since you are not always writing for the same target audience, you should tailor the attribution as well as the story itself. Here are two examples of attributions I added to my own articles, both of which were printed as I wrote them.

- This wording was attached to an article on business writing skills in a subscription newsletter aimed at law firms and individual lawyers specializing in litigation. My objective was to gain more clients for my in-house communication seminars for lawyers and to make them aware of my other speaking services:

  Helen Wilkie is a writer, speaker and consultant with MHW Communications of Toronto. She speaks at conferences and other events across Canada on topics relating to clear business communication, and has presented her full-length seminars to many major Canadian law firms. You can reach her at (416) 966-5023.

- The following attribution appeared after an article on presentation skills in the magazine of a national accounting association. My objective here was to publicize my speaking services on this topic:

  Helen Wilkie is a speaker, writer and consultant with MHW Communications of Toronto. She conducts in-house seminars across Canada on presentation skills, as well as a short program entitled "Helen's 9 Rules for Pithy Presentations". For information, contact her at (416) 966-5023; e-mail: mhwcomm@total.net.

Both of these brought immediate inquiries. Remember too that some people who don't have a need for you immediately but anticipate a need in the future will often keep the article on file. I have had calls from people who saw my name on an article two years before, and kept it on file until they needed me.

Because you don't always get the attribution you want, and in fact some publications give no more than your name, you should consider another popular method of making people contact you: offer them free information. This should be something that relates to the topic that can be assembled on one or two pages. For example, if you are a real estate agent, you might put together a checklist to help first-time home buyers remember the main items to look for in the properties they consider. That would be of value to them. Simply mention as part of your article that they can obtain this checklist by contacting you, and provide your phone, fax or e-mail information. One caveat here: magazines will often ask to see a copy of the item you are offering. They will not allow you to use this as an excuse to send out your promotional literature. It must be an item of information and value to readers.

Now, you have probably put a great deal of effort into researching and writing your article, so you want to get the most promotional mileage out of it. That brings us to ...

Rule No. 9: Recycle your articles

Even if you follow these tips for writing your articles, it's still a lot of work. If you need to research your subject, it's an even bigger investment of your time. If you value your time, you will want to get as much use out of this article as you can. An important way of doing that is to recycle the material by adapting it to fit other publications.

To give yourself as much freedom as possible in using your material, you should offer the publication one-time rights only. Depending on where you are, you might offer First North American Rights, One-time U.K. Rights or whatever is appropriate. This means after the publication has used your story, rights revert to you and you may market it again if you wish. While some publications insist on All Rights to published materials, most are happy to use your material once. Their policy on rights will be spelled out in their Writers' Guidelines, and you must respect that policy.

When submitting your manuscript, you should type the words *First North American Rights*, underlined, at the top of the first page. This clearly sets out your right to reuse your material.

So, why is this so important? How do you use it again? Get out the old reliable C.A.R.D. again, and look for other publications that could also be interested in your article. Of course, they must be publications that might be read by your target audience, but it is important that they are not competitors of the magazine that first published your story. Of course, you can no longer offer "first rights" to the story, so you now offer "one-time" rights.

You can widen the net even further if you look at ways to change the angle of your story for another market. For example, as a medical professional you might write a piece on asthma for a medical journal. Think about then taking out the professional jargon and finding an angle that would make it appropriate for a parenting magazine, talking about asthma in children. For those who suffer from it, asthma can be particularly bothersome when flying, so what about giving some tips on how to minimize the effects of air travel and selling it to in-flight magazines? You can see how it works. You have spent a lot of time on this, so get as much mileage as you can from it.

Let's assume you are successful in publishing a story in a magazines. How can you make it work for you? First, of course, it will be seen by the magazine's readers. If you are lucky, you may even receive calls based on your attribution. But you can make sure the article works for you by obtaining and sending out reprints. Many magazines offer specially prepared reprints of your article, on the same slick paper they use for the publication. These make a great addition to press kits, promotional materials and other information packets you send out to various audiences. Suppose you have been wooing a potential client for some time but haven't quite managed to get them to buy. It's more than possible that timely receipt of a published article that illustrates your expertise could be just the final push needed to move the person from prospect to client.

People are impressed when they know you have published, so it's worth every minute it takes, and it's not difficult if you just follow *Helen's 9 Rules for Publishable Prose*.

Helen's 9 Rules for Publishable Prose

1. *Target the publication before you write the article.*
2. *Plan your article for those particular readers.*
3. *Query first.*
4. *Tap the power of the formula.*
5. *Use appropriate language.*
6. *Remember it's a story.*
7. *Don't fight the editor.*
8. *Ask for full attribution.*
9. *Recycle your articles.*

In closing

So there you have it. These are *Helen's 9 Rules* for each of five areas of communication. Depending on your present skill level and your particular interests, no doubt you'll find some more useful than others, but I urge you to study them all.

They say it takes twenty-one days for a new habit to take hold. I suggest you begin with one set of *Helen's 9 Rules*—the one most important to you—and post it at your work station. Try to introduce the rules one at a time into the way you do your work, and give each rule at least twenty-one days to settle. As the new techniques become habit for you, you will not only communicate more effectively, but it will be less of a chore than before.

The Communication Contract© is real. Millions of business people are frustrated by their lack of ability to get their messages across, not realizing that they are fulfilling only one side of the contract. Remember, for every outgoing message, someone must receive and understand it. If we are all talking at once and no-one is listening, it's just noise.

Only when we are sure that both sides of the contract have been fulfilled can we truly say, ***"Message Received and Understood!"***

Index

A

acknowledgement 78
Active Voice 29
advertising 89
affirmation *67*
agenda 102, 106
All Rights 146
angle 128
appropriate language 135
Architectural Digest 135
arm's length test *56*
attitude 139
attribution 143

B

bandwagon 89
Be nice 33
best seat 117
Better Business Writing 11
Better Homes and Gardens 135
bite-sized pieces *48*
Body Language *62*
Body language 85
Broadening 83
Burst the Bubble 133
business correspondence 11
butterflies *65*

C

C.A.R.D. 125, 128, 146
call to action *46*
captive audience *42*
Changing direction 84
charts *54*
Chatelaine 135
cheatsheets *51*, *59*
Chronological *49*
Clarifying 83
clear objective *40*
clock *60*
close *45*
closed question 81
Communication Contract 95
congruent 87
Connect *61*
context 25
critics 113

D

Decide 74
deep breathing *65*
Definite article 20
detective fiction 131
Discussions 115
Divine Passive 30
draft 140

E

Economist, The 135
editor 142
Elements of Style 25
emotional response 91
errors 140
exploratory phrase 79
Expression *62*
Eye Contact *61*
eye contact *51*

F

facial expression *62*
fact checkers 142
feedback 78
financial statements *54*, *57*
Finish *58*
First North American Rights 146
flipframes *52*
fluff 17
formula 132
formulas *49*
full bleed 13

G

GAAP 13
gender neutral language 19
George Bernard Shaw 11
gestures *63*
Goal/roadmap *50*
grammar 22
Grammarcheck 31
graphs *54*
great pitch *39*
great quote *47*

H

handouts *57*
hands *63*
hard drive *44*
Hearing 73
Honey 34
hook *41*, 128
hot buttons 91

I

Imperative form 22
Index cards *52*
insurance regulations 127
Internet 88
Interview, The 134
intestate 13

J

jargon 12
journalist 123

L

laproscopic procedure 13
laser pointer *56*
Law of Primacy and Recency *41*
lead 138
length of your paragraphs 140
library *43*
lifestyle advertising 89
List, The 132
listening 73

M

major points *46*

meeting leader 102
meetings 97
Memorize *44*
Mental Remedies *66*
middle management meeting 98
minute taking 118

N

Names *64*
necessary meetings 100
non-verbal cues 84
non-verbal response 78
notes 93, 118

O

Objections/answers *50*
objective 111
Old way/new way *50*
Olivier, Sir Laurence *67*
one-time rights 146
One-time U.K. Rights 146
open question 81
opening *42*
opinion and propaganda 88
Oxford University Press 21

P

Passive Voice 30
Pericles *69*
personal pronoun 20
personal stories 138
Physical Remedies *65*
pie chart *55*
pitch *62*
Pithy Presentations *40*
Plan your article 127
plural form 19
Plural pronoun 20
Potential conflicts 101
power of the formula 131
President Bush *60*
Problem/solution *49*
provocative question *43*
provocative questions *42*
Publishable Prose 123

Q

Query 128
questions 81
quotations *44*

R

Rainmakers 123
rambling sentences 32
rapport *61*
Recycle 145
Redbook 135
redundant words 18
Reflective Listening 80
Regular Passive 30
rehearsal *68*
Rehearse *68*
Repetition 140
rhythm of your sentences 140
right people 103

S

S.R.D.S. 125, 128
sample issue 126, 135
sample query letter 129

Second person 21
selective listening 76
Short Case Studies 133
sidebar 139
simple words 14
Smile *62*
speaking muscles *66*
speech *51*
spellcheck 28
stagefright *65*, *67*
startling fact *43*
Startling facts *42*
Strunk and White 25
Style 140
subscription newsletter 144
Surveys and Studies 134
Sydney J. Harris *vii*
syntax 23

T

Target the publication 124
tension *66*
term life 13
The Communication Contract© *vii*
three-ring binder *52*
time waster 102
timing plan *58*
timing sheet *58*
tipsheets 126
tone 33
Tone of voice 86
tone of voice 85
tongue-twister *66*
Topical *51*
Translate *44*
transparency *56*
Trends *55*

V

Vinegar 34
visual aids *56*
visualization *67*
visualize *66*
visuals *53*
volunteer committee 109
vote 115

W

Wall Street Journal 135
Wasted words 140
What's in it for me *42*
word charts *55*
wordy phrases 17
Worldwide Web 89
Write for your reader 12
Writers' Guidelines 146
writers' guidelines 126

Helen Wilkie presents keynote speeches and in-house workshops on the following topics:

Speeches

- Message Received and Understood!
- Now Go **DO** It!
- Communication: the engine that drives the team
- Better sales through better communication
- Great customer service means great communication
- The fine art of conference networking

Skill-building programs for conference breakouts

- Helen's 9 Rules for Better Business Writing
- Helen's 9 Rules for Pithy Presentations
- Helen's 9 Rules for Lively Listening
- Helen's 9 Rules for Meaningful Meetings
- Helen's 9 Rules for Publishable Prose
- Helen's 9 Rules for Winning Websites

Workshops

- Effective Business Writing
- Get to Grips with Grammar!
- DESIGN IT©—a simple plan for easier report writing
- How to Make the Great Pitch (Presentation Skills)
- Message Received and Understood!—the workshop

For more information on Helen's speaking services, contact: